T0230092

Lecture Notes in Computer Science

Vol. 270: E. Börger (Ed.), Computation Theory and Logic. IX, 442 pages. 1987.

Vol. 271: D. Snyers, A. Thayse, From Logic Design to Logic Programming. IV, 125 pages. 1987.

Vol. 272: P. Treleaven, M. Vanneschi (Eds.), Future Parallel Computers. Proceedings, 1986. V, 492 pages. 1987.

Vol. 273: J.S. Royer, A Connotational Theory of Program Structure. V, 186 pages. 1987.

Vol. 274: G. Kahn (Ed.), Functional Programming Languages and Computer Architecture. Proceedings. VI, 470 pages. 1987.

Vol. 275: A.N. Habermann, U. Montanari (Eds.), System Development and Ada. Proceedings, 1986. V, 305 pages. 1987.

Vol. 276: J. Bézivin, J.-M. Hullot, P. Cointe, H. Lieberman (Eds.), ECOOP '87. European Conference on Object-Oriented Programming. Proceedings. VI, 273 pages. 1987.

Vol. 277: B. Benninghofen, S. Kemmerich, M.M. Richter, Systems of Reductions. X, 265 pages. 1987.

Vol. 278: L. Budach, R.G. Bukharajev, O.B. Lupanov (Eds.), Fundamentals of Computation Theory. Proceedings, 1987. XIV, 505 pages. 1987.

Vol. 279: J.H. Fasel, R.M. Keller (Eds.), Graph Reduction. Proceedings, 1986. XVI, 450 pages. 1987.

Vol. 280: M. Venturini Zilli (Ed.), Mathematical Models for the Semantics of Parallelism. Proceedings, 1986. V, 231 pages. 1987.

Vol. 281: A. Kelemenová, J. Kelemen (Eds.), Trends, Techniques, and Problems in Theoretical Computer Science. Proceedings, 1986. VI, 213 pages. 1987.

Vol. 282: P. Gorny, M.J. Tauber (Eds.), Visualization in Programming. Proceedings, 1986. VII, 210 pages. 1987.

Vol. 283: D.H. Pitt, A. Poigné, D.E. Rydeheard (Eds.), Category Theory and Computer Science. Proceedings, 1987. V, 300 pages. 1987.

Vol. 284: A. Kündig, R.E. Bührer, J. Dähler (Eds.), Embedded Systems. Proceedings, 1986. V, 207 pages. 1987.

Vol. 285: C. Delgado Kloos, Semantics of Digital Circuits. IX, 124 pages. 1987.

Vol. 286: B. Bouchon, R.R. Yager (Eds.), Uncertainty in Knowledge-Based Systems. Proceedings, 1986. VII, 405 pages. 1987.

Vol. 287: K.V. Nori (Ed.), Foundations of Software Technology and Theoretical Computer Science. Proceedings, 1987. IX, 540 pages. 1987.

Vol. 288: A. Blikle, MetaSoft Primer. XIII, 140 pages. 1987.

Vol. 289: H.K. Nichols, D. Simpson (Eds.), ESEC '87. 1st European Software Engineering Conference. Proceedings, 1987. XII, 404 pages. 1987.

Vol. 290: T.X. Bui, Co-oP A Group Decision Support System for Cooperative Multiple Criteria Group Decision Making. XIII, 250 pages. 1987.

Vol. 291: H. Ehrig, M. Nagl, G. Rozenberg, A. Rosenfeld (Eds.), Graph-Grammars and Their Application to Computer Science. VIII, 609 pages. 1987.

Vol. 292: The Munich Project CIP. Volume II: The Program Transformation System CIP-S. By the CIP System Group. VIII, 522 pages. 1987.

Vol. 293: C. Pomerance (Ed.), Advances in Cryptology — CRYPTO '87. Proceedings. X, 463 pages. 1988.

Vol. 294: R. Cori, M. Wirsing (Eds.), STACS 88. Proceedings, 1988. IX, 404 pages. 1988.

Vol. 295: R. Dierstein, D. Müller-Wichards, H.-M. Wacker (Eds.), Parallel Computing in Science and Engineering. Proceedings, 1987. V, 185 pages. 1988.

Vol. 296: R. Janßen (Ed.), Trends in Computer Algebra. Proceedings, 1987. V, 197 pages. 1988.

Vol. 297: E.N. Houstis, T.S. Papatheodorou, C.D. Polychronopoulos (Eds.), Supercomputing. Proceedings, 1987. X, 1093 pages. 1988.

Vol. 298: M. Main, A. Melton, M. Mislove, D. Schmidt (Eds.), Mathematical Foundations of Programming Language Semantics. Proceedings, 1987. VIII, 637 pages. 1988.

Vol. 299: M. Dauchet, M. Nivat (Eds.), CAAP '88. Proceedings, 1988. VI, 304 pages. 1988.

Vol. 300: H. Ganzinger (Ed.), ESOP '88. Proceedings, 1988. VI, 381 pages. 1988.

Vol. 301: J. Kittler (Ed.), Pattern Recognition. Proceedings, 1988. VII, 668 pages. 1988.

Vol. 302: D.M. Yellin, Attribute Grammar Inversion and Source-to-source Translation. VIII, 176 pages. 1988.

Vol. 303: J.W. Schmidt, S. Ceri, M. Missikoff (Eds.), Advances in Database Technology — EDBT '88. X, 620 pages. 1988.

Vol. 304: W.L. Price, D. Chaum (Eds.), Advances in Cryptology — EUROCRYPT '87. Proceedings, 1987. VII, 314 pages. 1988.

Vol. 305: J. Biskup, J. Demetrovics, J. Paredaens, B. Thalheim (Eds.), MFDBS 87. Proceedings, 1987. V, 247 pages. 1988.

Vol. 306: M. Boscarol, L. Carlucci Aiello, G. Levi (Eds.), Foundations of Logic and Functional Programming. Proceedings, 1986. V, 218 pages. 1988.

Vol. 307: Th. Beth, M. Clausen (Eds.), Applicable Algebra, Error-Correcting Codes, Combinatorics and Computer Algebra. Proceedings, 1986. VI, 215 pages. 1988.

Vol. 308: S. Kaplan, J.-P. Jouannaud (Eds.), Conditional Term Rewriting Systems. Proceedings, 1987. VI, 278 pages. 1988.

Vol. 309: J. Nehmer (Ed.), Experiences with Distributed Systems. Proceedings, 1987. VI, 292 pages. 1988.

Vol. 310: E. Lusk, R. Overbeek (Eds.), 9th International Conference on Automated Deduction. Proceedings, 1988. X, 775 pages. 1988.

Vol. 311: G. Cohen, P. Godlewski (Eds.), Coding Theory and Applications 1986. Proceedings, 1986. XIV, 196 pages. 1988.

Vol. 312: J. van Leeuwen (Ed.), Distributed Algorithms 1987. Proceedings, 1987. VII, 430 pages. 1988.

Vol. 313: B. Bouchon, L. Saitta, R.R. Yager (Eds.), Uncertainty and Intelligent Systems. IPMU '88. Proceedings, 1988. VIII, 408 pages. 1988.

Vol. 314: H. Göttler, H.J. Schneider (Eds.), Graph-Theoretic Concepts in Computer Science. Proceedings, 1987. VI, 254 pages. 1988.

Vol. 315: K. Furukawa, H. Tanaka, T. Fujisaki (Eds.), Logic Programming '87. Proceedings, 1987. VI, 327 pages. 1988.

Vol. 316: C. Choffrut (Ed.), Automata Networks. Proceedings, 1986. VII, 125 pages. 1988.

Vol. 317: T. Lepistö, A. Salomaa (Eds.), Automata, Languages and Programming. Proceedings, 1988. XI, 741 pages. 1988.

Vol. 318: R. Karlsson, A. Lingas (Eds.), SWAT 88. Proceedings, 1988. VI, 262 pages. 1988.

Vol. 319: J.H. Reif (Ed.), VLSI Algorithms and Architectures — AWOC 88. Proceedings, 1988. X, 476 pages. 1988.

Vol. 320: A. Blaser (Ed.), Natural Language at the Computer. Proceedings, 1988. III, 176 pages. 1988.

Vol. 321: J. Zwiers, Compositionality, Concurrency and Partial Correctness. VI, 272 pages. 1989.

Vol. 322: S. Gjessing, K. Nygaard (Eds.), ECOOP '88. European Conference on Object-Oriented Programming. Proceedings, 1988. VI, 410 pages. 1988.

Vol. 323: P. Deransart, M. Jourdan, B. Lorho, Attribute Grammars. IX, 232 pages. 1988.

Lecture Notes in Computer Science

Edited by G. Goos and J. Hartmanis

373

T. Theoharis

Algorithms for
Parallel Polygon Rendering

Springer-Verlag
Berlin Heidelberg New York London Paris Tokyo HongKong

Author

Theoharis Theoharis
St. Catherine's College
Cambridge CB2 1RL, UK

CR Subject Classification (1987): C.1.2, I.3.7

ISBN 3-540-51394-9 Springer-Verlag Berlin Heidelberg New York
ISBN 0-387-51394-9 Springer-Verlag New York Berlin Heidelberg

© Springer-Verlag Berlin Heidelberg 1989
Printed in Germany

Printing and binding: Druckhaus Beltz, Hemsbach/Bergstr.
2145/3140-543210 – Printed on acid-free paper

Preface

Research into algorithms and architectures for the support of high-performance graphics operations has a history of over ten years. Among the first researchers in this field were J. Clark (Geometry Engine), H. Fuchs (multiprocessor z-buffer and, later on, Pixel-planes) Ian Page (DisArray) and R. Sproull (8x8 display). Several special purpose graphics architectures have been proposed and they all have one common feature: they incorporate parallelism.

The availability of general purpose parallel processors such as the ICL DAP and systems based on the INMOS transputer is rapidly increasing. These machines are often used in scientific simulations producing large amounts of data, and efficient graphics support is necessary in order to display such data interactively. Still others use them in purely graphical applications, such as animation and flight simulation, and then the necessity for interactive graphics performance is even greater. The research necessary in order to satisfy the demands of such applications involves the design of graphics algorithms for parallel machines and this differs in nature from the design of special purpose hardware which can support existing algorithms.

In the last few years there has been a surge of interest in the use of general purpose parallel processors for graphics. Image synthesis is the common basis of many computationally expensive applications and this book deals with the implementation of polygon rendering techniques on a certain class of general purpose parallel processor. Polygonal modelling may not be the most favoured modelling technique nowadays but it is still the one that is most widely used due to its simplicity and generality and the fact that, although expensive in absolute terms, polygon rendering is computationally much cheaper than ray tracing, the other rendering technique.

The research reported here was based on the Disputer which incorporates a Multiple Instruction Multiple Data stream (MIMD) transputer network and a DAP-like Single Instruction Multiple Data stream (SIMD) processor array in a single architecture; this allows us to investigate SIMD, MIMD or even dual-paradigm algorithms. A review of certain milestone graphics architectures is presented in the introductory Chapter, followed by an informal description of the Disputer and its programming environment in Chapter 2. The next two Chapters mainly deal with polygon rendering on SIMD processor arrays. Chapter 3 describes how a processor array can perform polygon rendering operations based on the evaluation of linear functions. It discusses how linear functions can be efficiently evaluated on such a machine by using incremental computation where possible and minimising the initialisation cost. This is followed by an algorithm which uses precomputed surface patches in order to construct arbitrary instances of a restricted class of convex polygon (Chapter 4); precomputation trades space for time. Chapter 5 presents a polygon rendering method for the Disputer; the SIMD part of the Disputer is used almost exclusively for pixel-level operations while the rest of the work is delegated to the MIMD part. Apart from being a useful polygon rendering technique for Disputers (!) it is also an example of programming such a dual-paradigm machine efficiently. Chapter 6 contrasts two current instances of a SIMD and a MIMD machine in the context of the polygon clipping operation; some of the problems involved in comparing such diverse classes of machines are also discussed.

Acknowledgements. This book was originally a doctoral thesis and I would like to thank my supervisor, Ian Page, for always being so enthusiastic, Phil Winder for upgrading DisArray to the Disputer, Drs J. Sanders and N. Wiseman and Professors J. Diamessis and D. Parkinson for their comments on earlier drafts, the QMC Centre for Parallel Computing for the use of their DAP and all the friends and colleagues at the PRG for useful discussions. This project would not have been possible if it were not for the large amount of effort that Professor C.A.R. Hoare, Dr K. Cranstoun and Ian Page put into organising a financing scheme. The sources of this scheme were INMOS Ltd, Sigmex Ltd, the Pirie-Reid fund and Wolfson College, Oxford. The award of the Bibby Research Fellowship by St Catharine's College, Cambridge enables me to continue the pursuit of my academic interests. I would finally like to express my admiration for the responsible upbringing that my parents offered me which helped me to make the right decisions at the beginning of my career.

T. Theoharis

Cambridge
June 1989

To Maureen

Contents

1 Introduction 1

1.1 The Goal 1
1.2 Display Technology 1
1.3 The Graphics Output Pipeline 3
1.3.1 Filling 5
1.3.2 Hidden Surface Elimination 6
1.3.3 Smooth Shading 7
1.3.4 Anti-aliasing 8
1.4 The Need for Parallelism 9
1.5 Parallel Approaches to Rendering - Related Work 10
1.6 Overview 15

2 Graphics on General Purpose Parallel Architectures 17

2.1 Introduction 17
2.2 DisArray and the DAP 18
2.3 Mapping the Frame Buffer Onto a Processor Array 22
2.4 Occam and the Transputer 24
2.5 The Disputer 25
2.6 Planar Operations 26
2.6.1 Broadcast 28
2.6.2 Planar Assignment 29
2.6.3 Planar Arithmetic and Boolean Operations 29
2.6.4 Planar Comparison 30
2.6.5 Planar Shift 30
2.7 Conclusion 31

3 A Parallel Incremental Rendering Method 32

3.1 Introduction 32
3.2 Incremental Filling on a Processor Array 33
3.2.1 Incremental Polygon Filling Algorithm 33
3.2.2 Efficient Evaluation of the Linear Function on a Processor Array ... 34
3.2.3 Accuracy of Representation 39
3.2.4 Visiting Only Intersecting Windows 40
3.2.5 Processor Utilisation in Linear Function Evaluation 41
3.2.6 Performance 43
3.2.7 Word- versus Bit-Parallelism 45
3.3 Incremental Hidden Surface Elimination on a Processor Array ... 46
3.4 Texturing and Shading 48

3.4.1   Texture Mapping   48
3.4.2   Incremental Smooth Shading on a Processor Array   49
3.5   Merging Fill, HSE and SS   51
3.6   Anti-aliasing   52
3.6.1   Anti-aliasing by Normalisation of $F(x,y){=}ax{+}by{+}c$ 52
3.6.2   Anti-aliasing by Change of Resolution   53
3.7   Non-Linear Functions: Evaluation on a Processor Array and Rendering Usage   57
3.7.1   Filling Curved Convex Areas   59
3.7.2   Hidden Surface Elimination of Non-Planar Surfaces   60
3.8   Comparison With Other Rendering Systems   61
3.9   Conclusion   64

4   **Parallel Polygon Rendering With Precomputed Surface Patches** **65**

4.1   Introduction   65
4.2   Two Approaches and Our Choice   66
4.2.1   The Patch-First Approach   67
4.2.2   The RW-First Approach   68
4.3   The RW-First Algorithm   70
4.3.1   Order of Visiting the RW's   71
4.4   The N-step Line Generating Algorithm   72
4.5   How Many Surface Patches?   78
4.6   Performance   80
4.7   Texture Mapping   83
4.8   Anti-aliasing the Surface Patches   83
4.9   Is Precomputation of the Values of a Linear Function Feasible?   84
4.10   Precomputed Spheres   85
4.11   Conclusion   85

5   **Parallel Polygon Rendering on a Dual-Paradigm Parallel Processor** **87**

5.1   Introduction   87
5.2   Convex Polygon Filling on the Disputer   88
5.2.1   The Communication Protocol   89
5.2.2   Subwindow Polygon Rendering on a Processor Array   90
5.2.3   Splitting Polygons Into Subwindow Polygons- Determination of the Surface Patches   94
5.3   Performance   98
5.3.1   Processor Array Rendering Performance   98
5.3.2   Rendering Versus Splitting Performance 100
5.3.3   Communication Cost 104
5.4   Hidden Surface Elimination on the Disputer 104
5.4.1   Hidden Surface Elimination on the Processor Array 105
5.4.2   Hidden Surface Elimination on a Transputer Pipeline 105
5.5   Further Extensions of the Renderer / Splitter System 110
5.6   Conclusion 111

6   **Control Parallel Versus Data Parallel Polygon Clipping** **112**

6.1   Introduction 112
6.2   Estimating Performance 113
6.3   The Sutherland-Hodgman Polygon Clipping Algorithm 114
6.3.1   Key Clipping Calculations 116
6.3.2   Scope for Parallelism 118
6.4   A Control Parallel Implementation of the Sutherland-Hodgman Algorithm 119
6.4.1   Description of the Control Parallel Implementation 119

6.4.2   Performance of the Control Parallel Implementation 121
6.5   A Data Parallel Implementation of the Sutherland-Hodgman Algorithm 122
6.5.1   Distribution of the Polygon Vertices 122
6.5.2   Description of the Data Parallel Implementation 124
6.5.3   Performance of the Data Parallel Implementation 129
6.5.4   Usefulness of the Data Parallel Implementation 129
6.6   Contrasting the Two Parallel Implementations 130
6.7   Conclusion 131

7   Conclusion 132

7.1   Contribution of this Work 132
7.2   Discussion 132
7.3   Further Work 134

A 1   Implementation of Planar Operations 135

A 2   Implementation of Control Parallel Clipper 138

A 3   Implementation of Data Parallel Clipper 141

References 143

Abbreviations

FB: Frame Buffer

ZB: z-Buffer (Depth Buffer)

PE: Processing Element

SIMD: Single Instruction Multiple Data stream

MIMD: Multiple Instruction Multiple Data stream

HSE: Hidden Surface Elimination

SS: Smooth Shading

RW: Relevant Window

2D: Two Dimensional

3D: Three Dimensional

Symbols

I: Size if the side of image space. Square $I \times I$ image space assumed. I is assumed to be a multiple of N.

N: Size of the side of the processor array. Square $N \times N$ processor array assumed. $N > 1$ and a power of 2.

M: Depth of the processor array (bit-parallelism). $M \geq 1$.

fd: Depth of frame buffer in bits.

zd: Depth of z-buffer in bits.

pd: Depth of planar arithmetic representation in bits.

P: Number of polygons to be processed.

p: Number of pixels in a polygon.

n: Number of sides of a polygon. $n \geq 3$.

w: Number of relevant windows. $w \geq 1$.

s: Number of polygon side / window intersections. $s \geq 3$.

Chapter 1
Introduction

1.1. The Goal

Ivan Sutherland is considered as the father of computer graphics due to his work on "Sketchpad" which took place as early as 1963 [Suth63]. Two years later he tried to predict the future of computer graphics by describing his vision of the "ultimate display" [Suth65]. This display would be able to produce images so realistic that they would be indistinguishable to the viewer from real scenes. In fact the "ultimate display" provided for inputs to all of our five senses, not just sight, but we shall not be concerned with the rest here!

In the field of computer graphics two main research paths have been taken towards the goal of the "ultimate display". The first one leads to the set of techniques required in order to create realistic scenes and the second one involves algorithms and architectures necessary to support the above techniques efficiently i.e. display successive images (*frames*) on a graphical output device in rapid succession (at least 30 frames per second) in order to give the illusion of real-time motion. We are concerned with the latter theme of research.

Although the "ultimate display" is still distant, there exist applications that have successfully used the fruits of ongoing research in the field. Flight simulation and CAD/CAM systems are two representative examples of applications that require the generation of realistic, real-time images. Current systems are very expensive (flight simulator costs are of the order of millions of pounds) and the desire for performance beyond their capabilities exists.

1.2. Display Technology

There is a wide variety of graphics output devices, see for example [Fole83], but we shall only be concerned with the *frame-buffer-refreshed raster-scan-display*. The display is the familiar television screen whose surface is subdivided into a 2D array of individually addressable picture elements (*pixels*). Each pixel can take on a range of colours. The screen is refreshed at a rate of at least 30 Hz (to avoid flicker) from a large memory which contains one location for the storage of the colour of every pixel on the screen.

2

This memory is called the *frame buffer* and its size is of the order of 1 Mbyte in modern high resolution graphics systems. The screen refresh is carried out in a particular order called *raster-scan*. *Frame-buffer-refreshed raster-scan-displays* (shortened to raster-scan displays) are the most popular graphics output device in use today for the following reasons:

1. They use cheap television technology.
2. They are more suitable for the display of filled areas than *vector-scan* displays which can only display vectors. (Some fast, but expensive, vector-scan systems can simulate filled areas by using a large number of vectors).
3. The cost of the memory required for the frame buffer is now low and continuously falling.
4. They can be used to produce an arbitrary image by properly recording the colour of every pixel in the frame buffer.

The usual arrangement of a graphics system using a raster-scan display is shown in figure 1.1.

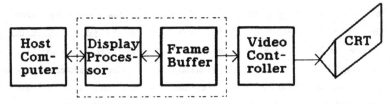

Figure 1.1. Graphics display system with frame buffer

The *video controller* is assigned the sole task of refreshing the cathode-ray tube (CRT) from the frame buffer. The frame buffer is usually constructed out of dual-ported memories i.e. memories that can be accessed via two different ports. The recent advent of video RAMs [Form85] has further simplified the construction of frame buffers and reduced the number of frame buffer memory cycles required for video refresh. A video RAM is a dual-ported memory that contains a long shift register which can be loaded from the RAM in one cycle and then "clocked" to provide the video output. The video output is thus provided in parallel with updates to the RAM.

The *display processor* updates the contents of the frame buffer according to the commands it receives from the *host computer*. For example the host computer may send the coordinates of the vertices of a polygon to the display processor which then updates all the frame buffer locations that correspond to pixels within the polygon to the value that represents the polygon's colour. The task of the display processor is called *scan conversion* or, in the more general case which includes such tasks as smooth shading and anti-aliasing (to be described in due course), *rendering*.

From now on we shall restrict our attention to the display processor and the frame buffer (enclosed in the dotted line in figure 1.1). The problem of video generation has been satisfactorily solved (in time performance terms) as explained above and rendering is the performance bottleneck in current graphics display systems. Graphics operations other than rendering, such as clipping and coordinate transformations to be described in §1.3, are computationally cheaper than the rendering operation.

1.3. The Graphics Output Pipeline

The scene to be displayed is modelled by instances of a set of primitives and stored in the host computer's memory or a special purpose data-base (the planar polygon is the most common primitive because of its generality and we shall mainly be concerned with polygons). The polygons, which are defined in an arbitrary 3D coordinate system called *world coordinate system* (X_w, Y_w, Z_w), are subjected to a sequence of operations which eventually transform them into a 2D image on the display screen. The sequence of operations is shown in figure 1.2.

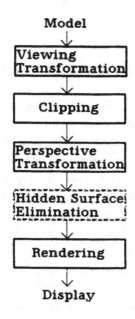

Figure 1.2. The graphics output pipeline

Given an arbitrary view point and direction within the world coordinate system, the *viewing transformation* transforms the polygons into another 3D coordinate system whose origin is at the view point and whose z-axis lies along the direction of view; the new coordinate system is the *eye coordinate system* (X_e, Y_e, Z_e). The viewing transformation simplifies the task of subsequent operations. The coordinate systems used are shown in figure 1.3.

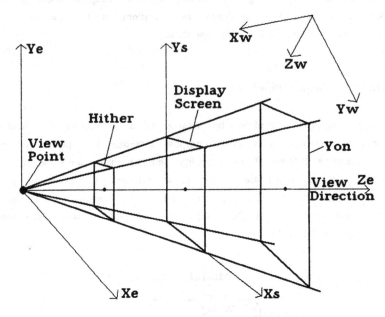

Figure 1.3. Coordinate systems and clipping pyramid

Clipping "filters out" polygons, or parts of polygons, that do not lie within a certain volume of eye coordinate space and thereby removes them from further consideration in subsequent operations. The clipping volume usually takes the form of a pyramid whose apex coincides with the view point, is symmetrical with respect to the z-axis of the eye coordinate system and each of its four faces is perpendicular to some pair of eye coordinate axes (see figure 1.3). The clipping pyramid is usually truncated by a pair of "hither" and "yon" planes which are perpendicular to the z-axis of the eye coordinate system and which impose depth restrictions on the polygons being clipped.

The *perspective transformation* follows the clipping operation and projects the polygons onto a 2D coordinate system called the *screen coordinate system* (X_s, Y_s) or *image space*, figure 1.3. The perspective transformation is depth preserving, i.e. it does not lose the depth information when projecting onto 2D, in order to enable the next operation, *hidden surface elimination* or HSE, to remove polygons, or parts of polygons, that are occluded by others. The perspective transformation transforms the truncated clipping pyramid into a cuboid (rectangular parallelepiped) thus simplifying comparisons between the x and y screen coordinates of polygons (such comparisons are used by HSE algorithms).

The final operation, *rendering*, transforms the mathematical descriptions of polygons (e.g. vertices plus colour information) into a frame buffer image. Rendering encompasses all the operations that access the frame buffer and the most fundamental of these operations is *scan conversion* or *filling* i.e. the identification of the pixels covered by a polygon.

1.3.1. Filling

To fill the area covered by a polygon we need to define a function which, given the coordinates of a pixel, produces a Boolean value which indicates whether the pixel is inside the area or not. Two functions suitable for filling polygons and convex polygons respectively are presented below:

1. The function which tests the parity of the number of intersections of the polygon boundary with a halfline from the pixel to infinity is a suitable polygon filling function. A pixel lying *on* the boundary is counted as an intersection if the boundary is to be included in the area of the polygon. In figure 1.4 halfline L_1 intersects the polygon boundary an odd number of times and therefore P_1 is inside the polygon while L_2 intersects the polygon boundary an even number of times and therefore P_2 is outside the polygon.

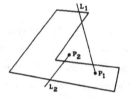

Figure 1.4. Polygon filling by counting the number of halfline intersections with polygon boundary

2. A convex polygon can be defined as the intersection of the n halfplanes defined by its n sides (including the sides themselves). Each side of the convex polygon lies on an infinite line, $ax+by+c=0$, which divides the plane into two halfplanes. If the coordinates of two pixels lying in opposite halfplanes are substituted into the function $F(x,y)=ax+by+c$, then the two resulting values will have opposite signs. Thus by deriving the coefficients of the line equations from the coordinates of pairs of vertices in a consistent manner (see §3.2.1), it is possible to ensure that the convex polygon will always lie on the "positive" halfplane of each line. (Whether the convex polygon lies on the "positive" or "negative" halfplane depends on the derivation of the line equation coefficients). It is therefore possible to decide whether a pixel is within a convex polygon by checking whether its coordinates give a non-negative value to each of the n functions defined by the convex polygon's sides. The filling function can thus be defined as the Boolean ANDing of the

(negations of the) signs of the above values. Figure 1.5 demonstrates this technique for a triangle. F_i is the function derived for side i.

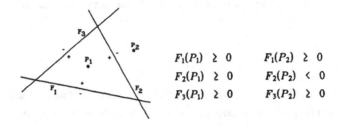

$$F_1(P_1) \geq 0 \qquad F_1(P_2) \geq 0$$
$$F_2(P_1) \geq 0 \qquad F_2(P_2) < 0$$
$$F_3(P_1) \geq 0 \qquad F_3(P_2) \geq 0$$

Figure 1.5. Convex polygon filling by halfplane intersection

Most filling algorithms do not fill polygons by testing *every* pixel using the above functions; instead they take advantage of *area coherence* i.e. the characteristic that adjacent pixels tend to be similar (as regards their containment in the polygon) in order to reduce the number of tests performed.

1.3.2. Hidden Surface Elimination

A large number of algorithms have been proposed for eliminating the hidden surfaces. HSE algorithms can be classified according to whether they deal with the mathematical descriptions of objects (e.g. polygons) or with the pixels that are contained in the image space projections of the objects. The former are called *object space* and the latter *image space* algorithms. A classic survey of HSE algorithms is [Suth74a]. The image space algorithms (such as the z-buffer presented below) can be regarded as part of the rendering operation; for this reason HSE is within dotted lines in figure 1.2. The following HSE algorithms are probably the simplest and most amenable to parallel implementation:

1. The *painter's algorithm* works in object space and attempts to order the polygons according to distance from the view point. The polygons are then rendered, starting from the one that is furthest away from the view point. Thus if polygon A is nearer to the view point than polygon B, A will be rendered after B and the colour of B will be overwritten by that of A in the (possible) area of overlap of the two polygons. The problem with this algorithm is that if the polygons' depth extents overlap, distance from the view point does not unambiguously indicate which polygon obscures the other. A sequence of tests of increasing complexity can be performed in order to resolve this ambiguity [Newe72]. In the worst case the polygons can not be ordered (see figure 5.9) and it is necessary to split them. An alternative way of resolving the ambiguity, is to impose appropriate restrictions on the relative locations of polygons which make the

"ordering key" (e.g. distance from the view point) unambiguous in the above sense [Will77, Will78]. The complexity of the painter's algorithm is $O(P \log P)$ i.e. the complexity of sorting P items (ignoring the cost of any extra ordering tests and polygon splits).

2. The $z\text{-}buffer\ algorithm$ [Suth74a] operates in image space. It uses a large memory (the z-buffer) which has one location for every pixel in image space. The z-buffer maintains the depth of the nearest polygon at each pixel. When filling a polygon, its depth is derived at each of the pixels it covers and compared against the z-buffer value for that pixel. If the depth of the polygon at a particular pixel is less than the z-buffer value for the same pixel, then the relevant z-buffer location is updated with the depth of the polygon and the corresponding frame buffer location takes the colour of the polygon. Otherwise, no action is taken. The complexity of the z-buffer algorithm is $O(Pp)$ where P is the number of polygons and p the average number of pixels in each polygon. Since the product Pp is insensitive to the number of polygons (if the number of polygons is increased, the average number of pixels per polygon is usually correspondingly reduced), the performance of the z-buffer algorithm is not sensitive to the number of polygons in the scene. Thus with decreasing memory costs (the z-buffer memory is of the order of 1 Mbyte) and increasing scene complexities (more polygons) the z-buffer algorithm continuously becomes more cost-effective.

1.3.3. Smooth Shading

Rendering can be extended to include a number of techniques (some of which are computationally very expensive) in order to enhance the realism of the image. The most common techniques are *smooth shading*, *texture mapping* and *anti-aliasing*. When a curved object is modelled by planar polygons each of which is assigned a constant colour intensity, intensity discontinuities will arise at the polygon boundaries. These discontinuities can be removed by varying the intensity over each polygon so that intensity values match at polygon boundaries. Such smooth shading techniques have been developed by Gouraud [Gour71] and Phong [Phon75].

Gouraud shading is based on intensity interpolation and it is a four step process. First the *surface normal* vectors to the polygons that make up an object are calculated. Then *vertex normals* are computed by averaging the surface normals of all polygons that share a vertex. Third, *vertex intensities* are estimated by using the vertex normals and the desired shading model. (A shading model is a function which produces the intensity of a surface at a particular point given such arguments as the normal vector of the surface at the point, the properties of the surface and the position, intensity and orientation of the light source(s)). Finally, after the polygons have been projected into 2D by the perspective transformation, linear interpolations of the vertex intensities along the edges and between the edges (along the scan lines), are used to shade each of the polygons. Notice that it is only the linear interpolations that are performed in image space and are part of the rendering operation. Figure 1.6 demonstrates the computation performed in the fourth step. The linear interpolations are performed incrementally.

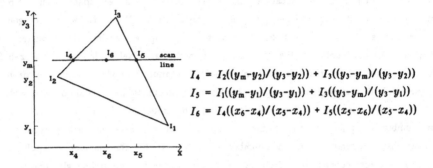

$$I_4 = I_2((y_m-y_2)/(y_3-y_2)) + I_3((y_3-y_m)/(y_3-y_2))$$
$$I_5 = I_1((y_m-y_1)/(y_3-y_1)) + I_3((y_3-y_m)/(y_3-y_1))$$
$$I_6 = I_4((x_6-x_4)/(x_5-x_4)) + I_5((x_5-x_6)/(x_5-x_4))$$

Figure 1.6. Gouraud shading. I_x stands for the intensity at point x

Phong shading is also a four step process based on vector interpolation. Steps 1 and 2 are the same as for Gouraud shading. However steps 3 and 4 are reversed. Instead of calculating vertex intensities using a shading model and then performing linear interpolation of these intensities within the polygon, Phong shading performs vector interpolation of the vertex normals and then uses the resulting vectors to calculate an intensity at every pixel within the polygon using the desired shading model.

Although Gouraud shading provides an acceptable smooth appearence, the results of Phong shading are superior because intensity does not always vary linearly in nature (consider highlight effects). However Phong shading is much more expensive computationally because the shading calculation is performed for every pixel within the polygon. For this reason Gouraud shading is the preferred shading method in high performance image generation systems.

Another rendering technique, texture mapping, can be used to accurately display objects whose surfaces are not smooth such as gravel roads and brick walls. The surfaces of such objects contain too much fine detail to be explicitly modelled using polygons.

1.3.4. Anti-aliasing

The discretisation involved in generating a raster image can give rise to aliasing, i.e. the failure to accurately reproduce a signal from digital samples when the sampling frequency is less than double the highest frequency in the signal (Nyquist's sampling theorem [Hamm77]).

The effects of aliasing appear as jagged edges or vanishing fine detail [Crow77]. Anti-aliasing techniques are used to mitigate these effects and they can be classified into two broad groups:

1. *Post-filtering* i.e. computing the image to a resolution which is higher than the resolution of the raster-scan display. (The sampling frequency is thus increased). The intensities of a local area of pixels of the high resolution image are then averaged to produce the intensity of a pixel in the low resolution image (the low resolution image has the resolution of the raster-scan display). Better results can be achieved by using a weighted average.

2. *Pre-filtering* i.e. considering each sample point (pixel) as a finite area rather than an infinitesimal spot. The intensity of the pixel is then computed by estimating an intensity contribution from each intersecting polygon based on the area of intersection.

Pre-filtering is computationally advantageous for scenes of low complexity (few polygons, no textures) while post-filtering is more advantageous for scenes of high complexity [Crow81].

For more information about the rendering operations see one of the textbooks on computer graphics: Newman & Sproull [Newm79], Foley & Van Dam [Fole83], Park [Park85] and Hearn & Baker [Hear86] are four popular texts.

1.4. The Need for Parallelism

The operations constituting the graphics output pipeline described in the previous section, must be performed on all the polygons that make up a scene as rapidly as possible for interactive applications. In the case of real-time display, e.g. flight simulators, the time constraint is about 30ms. Within this length of time, the operations defined by the graphics output pipeline must be performed on thousands of polygons (the order of 10,000 polygons for a complex scene). Even in non-interactive applications like computer generated films, the large number of frames to be produced makes speed very desirable.

If we assume that 1000 machine code instructions are required in order to perform all the operations on a single polygon (a very conservative estimate), then the computational power required to process 10,000 polygons 30 times per second would be of the order of 300 MIPS. Such performance is very expensive to achieve using current technology and the only way to provide it at reasonable cost is by the use of parallel processing. One has to identify tasks that can be performed in parallel and design the appropriate parallel algorithms and architectures. Better still, parallel algorithms may be developed for existing general purpose parallel architectures such as the transputer [INMO86] and the DAP [Redd73, Park83].

A first step in exploiting parallelism is to use a physical pipeline of processors each hosting a different stage of the graphics output pipeline. The polygons then "flow" through the pipeline of processors. Such pipeline systems have been designed by Clark [Clar82] and the author [Theo85]. Clark's system, the Geometry Engine, uses special purpose VLSI chips while the author's is based on general purpose transputers for the processors of the pipeline. In a pipeline of processors, one must ensure that the complexity of all the stages is approximately the same. Otherwise, the pipeline will run at the pace of the slowest stage and the processor utilisation will be low. (Processor utilisation is a measure of how busy we keep our processors and can be expressed as the ratio of useful execution time over total time). All the operations of the graphics output pipeline apart from rendering and HSE (i.e. clipping and the two coordinate transformations) have a time complexity which is proportional to the number of polygons to be processed. However the time complexity of rendering (including HSE if performed in image space) is proportional to the number of polygons times the average polygon area. Rendering thus represents a "bottleneck" in a pipeline implementation.

It is mainly because rendering represents a performance bottleneck in the graphics output pipeline that recent research efforts have concentrated on the design of parallel algorithms and architectures to support rendering. These parallel architectures usually distribute the frame buffer memory among the multiple processors; because there is no point in increasing the rate at which pixel values are calculated if the frame buffer does not have sufficient bandwidth to accept the pixel values at that rate. By partitioning the frame buffer among a number of processors which access the different partitions in parallel, the bandwidth of the frame buffer is increased.

1.5. Parallel Approaches to Rendering - Related Work

In this section we shall discuss the main parallel architectures and algorithms that have been proposed for the efficient execution of the rendering operation. The architectures presented in this section are special purpose in that they can be used for rendering only. According to Kilgour [Kilg85] there are two ways of dividing the rendering task among several processors:

i. The *"pixel serial"* (polygon parallel) approach distributes the polygons among the processors. Thus pixels are processed sequentially and polygons (or a subset of them) in parallel.

ii. The *"polygon serial"* (pixel parallel) approach distributes the pixels among the processors. In this case polygons are processed sequentially and pixels (or a subset of them) in parallel.

Most of the proposed architectures can be classified according to the above scheme. In what follows "host" will refer to the host of the graphics system plus the hardware that performs the operations of the graphics output pipeline apart from rendering. This may be a pipeline of processors as described in the previous section.

Clark and Hannah have proposed a polygon serial machine which assigns to each processor the responsibility for a particular set of pixels [Clar80]. The processors are purpose built in VLSI and organised as a 2D array with a second level of "column" processors assigned one per column of the array. Communication can only take place via a broadcast bus from a column processor to the processors of its column or from the "parent" processor to all the column processors (via a similar bus), see figure 1.7.

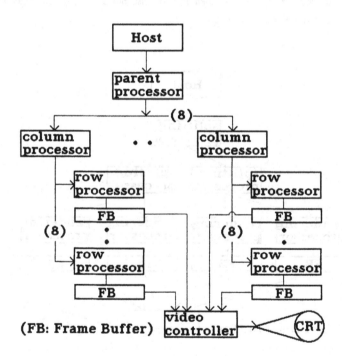

Figure 1.7. Clark and Hannah's system

The frame buffer memory is distributed among the "row" processors in an interlaced manner i.e. processor (i,j) | i,j: $0..N$-1 is responsible for pixels:

$$(i+mN, \quad j+nN) \quad | \quad m,n: 0..(I/N)\text{-}1$$

where I refers to the $I \times I$ pixel image- or screen-space and N refers to the $N \times N$ array of processors. This is called *sheet* mapping by Reddaway [Redd88]. This interlaced distribution of the frame buffer ensures that each of the processors will perform a roughly equivalent amount of work (compare this to Parke's system described below). Each processor executes the rendering operation for only the pixels of its responsibility. The same polygon is handled in parallel by all processors which operate asynchronously. When all processors have finished rendering a polygon, the host can broadcast the next polygon to be rendered. Fuchs has described a similar system in [Fuch77] and [Fuch79].

Parke describes another polygon serial machine which is different from Clark & Hannah's in the way the frame buffer memory is distributed among the processors [Park80]. In Parke's machine each processor is responsible for a contiguous block of pixels. Reddaway calls this *crinkled* mapping [Redd88]. A binary tree of splitting processors is then required in order to separate the polygons according to their image space coordinates, figure 1.8. An extension of the Sutherland-Hodgman polygon clipping algorithm [Suth74b] can be used to split polygons. If the frame buffer memory is distributed among m rendering processors then the splitter tree must have $\lceil \log_2 m \rceil$ levels.

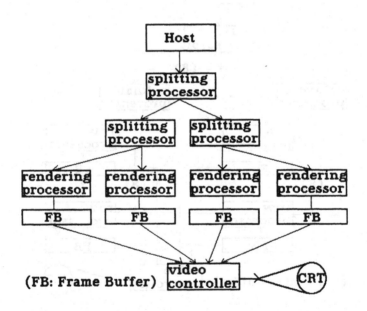

Figure 1.8. Parke's machine with 4 rendering processors

Parke's machine assumes that polygons are evenly distributed in image space. If they are not, some rendering processors will be underutilised. Parke also proposed a hybrid system that uses both sheet and crinkled mapping in an attempt to overcome the above problem.

Sproull et. al. have proposed the 8×8 display, a polygon serial architecture consisting of 8×8 processors each of which is assigned 1/64th of the frame buffer [Gupt8lb, Spro83]. As in Clark and Hannah's system, the frame buffer is sheet mapped (interlaced in both x and y) among the processors. The main contributions of the 8×8 display are the following:

1. The *square word* memory access geometry which treats long thin and short wide graphical primitives equivalently as opposed to conventional word geometries.

2. *Quadrant addressing*, that is, the ability to access arbitrarily aligned square words in 1 (rather than 4) memory cycles. This is achieved by providing different addresses to different memory chips.

3. The provision of a large *video buffer* for efficient video output from the 8×8 memory organisation. The size required for the video buffer is 16 scan-lines.

The geometry of the 8×8 display resembles that of the general purpose SIMD processor array presented in Chapter 2 and it seems that the rendering algorithms for the two machines would be similar. Gupta has shown how to draw lines on the 8×8 display using precomputed strokes of various slopes [Gupt8la] (a stroke is a line segment whose endpoints coincide with the boundaries of an 8×8 square). Line drawing has a potential speedup of N from the use of an $N{\times}N$ square array of processors (when compared to the performance of a uniprocessor). Polygon rendering has a potential speedup factor of N^2, but such algorithms have not yet been investigated and are the main theme of Chapters 3 and 4.

Pixel-planes, yet another polygon serial machine, has been suggested and built by Fuchs et. al. [Fuch81, Fuch85]. It uses a very simple processor at every pixel whose local memory stores the colour and depth of the nearest polygon at each pixel. The processors are thus very tightly coupled with the frame buffer memory. The processors are the leaves of a tree which can evaluate the linear function $F(x,y)=ax+by+c$ at all pixels $(x,y) \mid x,y:0..I-1$ simultaneously. A polygon is rendered by expressing the rendering operations in terms of linear function evaluations. First, the a, b and c coefficients of the equations of the lines defined by each edge of the polygon are used to evaluate the corresponding functions for all pixels in parallel and hence identify the pixels that are inside the polygon by the second filling method of §1.3.1. Of course, the above way of identifying the "inside" pixels is only applicable to convex polygons. The second step is the evaluation of another linear function whose result is the depth of the polygon's plane. Processors whose pixels were "inside" the polygon in step 1, compare the depth of the polygon at their pixel against the depth of the nearest previous polygon at that pixel. If the new depth is greater, they disable themselves otherwise they take part in step 3 which is the evaluation of yet another linear function resulting in the grey scale intensity of the polygon at each pixel (3 functions must be evaluated if colour shading is used). Processors that are still enabled after steps 1 and 2 change the intensity of their pixel to the new intensity. The above method of eliminating hidden surfaces is a parallel version of the z-buffer HSE algorithm described in §1.3.2. The main criticism of Pixel-planes is the low processor utilisation resulting from rendering small polygons. Fuchs, Goldfeather et. al. have also developed a generalisation of Pixel-planes which can evaluate quadratic functions [Gold86a, Gold86b]. The evaluation of quadratic functions can be used to display second-order curved surfaces such as those required for Constructive Solid Geometry.

Demetrescu has proposed another polygon serial system which closely couples processors and memory [Deme85]. The novelty of Demetrescu's rendering system lies in the Scan Line Access Memories (SLAM's) whose words are as wide as a scan-line (row of pixels). It is thus possible to update the part of the frame buffer that represents the portion of a row of pixels covered by a polygon in just one memory cycle. Demetrescu also describes how to incorporate texture maps and how to extend the system in order to handle smooth shading.

The next two systems are pixel serial, i.e. they process pixels sequentially and polygons in parallel by assigning a processor to each polygon. In doing so, they also try to eliminate the need for a frame buffer by processing pixels in the order they will have to be displayed and determining the colour of each pixel in the time interval between the display of successive pixels.

Cohen and Demetrescu have proposed a modular design consisting of one processor per polygon [Cohe81]. The processors, which are connected in a pipeline, incrementally determine whether each pixel in image space is inside their polygon and, if inside, the depth and colour of the polygon at that pixel. The incremental calculations are performed synchronously by all processors but, at any instant, adjacent processors in the pipeline are working on adjacent pixels (in raster-scan order). Descriptions of pixels consisting of the background colour and the maximum representable depth value are introduced at the beginning of the pipeline. When a processor receives a pixel description, it compares the incoming depth value with the depth of its own polygon at the corresponding pixel and, if the incoming depth value is larger (i.e. its own polygon is nearer to the viewpoint at the pixel), it updates the pixel description with the depth and colour of its own polygon at the pixel. The pixel description is finally output to the next processor in the pipeline. Pixel descriptions appearing at the end of the pipeline correspond to visible surfaces and the colour values of these pixel descriptions can be used to drive the display directly, see figure 1.9. The difficulty involved in the construction of the pipeline described above is in ensuring that a processor can process a pixel description in one pixel time (i.e. the interval between the display of successive pixels).

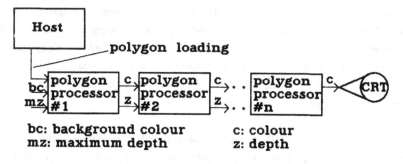

Figure 1.9. Cohen and Demetrescu's pipeline

Grimsdale's system is also pixel serial and assigns a zone management processor (ZMP) to each polygon [Grim79]. A ZMP delivers output signals when the CRT beam enters and leaves its polygon. For any scan-line, a separate ZMP is required for each polygon that intersects the scan-line. Every ZMP has a relative priority number which depends on the distance of the ZMP's polygon from the view point. Hidden surfaces are handled by a priority resolving circuit which, in case of contention, grants control of the CRT beam to the ZMP with the highest priority i.e. the ZMP whose polygon is nearest to the view point. This ZMP then sets the colour of the CRT beam to be that of its polygon.

To the best of our knowledge, none of the above rendering systems have so far reached the market place. The most probable reason behind this is that the application domain of special purpose systems is limited and their implementation cost is high. The marketed high performance graphics hardware does, however, increasingly rely on parallelism. The successful IRIS workstation for example [Akel88] originally used a pipeline of Clark's Geomerty Engines [Clar82] for clipping and coordinate transformations (these have now been replaced by Weitek chips). The rendering stage of IRIS is also implemented by a highly parallel set of custom designed chips.

1.6. Overview

Chapter 2 describes the general purpose parallel processor used for the implementation of the algorithms in subsequent Chapters. In particular we discuss the Single Instruction Multiple Data stream (SIMD) processor array, the Multiple Instruction Multiple Data stream (MIMD) transputer system, the Disputer (a SIMD-MIMD system constructed in Oxford) and our implementation of a set of operations on the SIMD part of the Disputer which provide an interface between the SIMD and the MIMD parts of the Disputer.

As mentioned in §1.5, polygon rendering algorithms for SIMD processor arrays have not yet been investigated by other researchers and they are the main subject of Chapters 3 and 4.

Chapter 3 presents a novel method for the efficient, incremental, evaluation of linear functions on SIMD processor arrays. It is shown how some polygon rendering operations can be implemented by translating them into linear function evaluations. Chapter 4 shows how the technique of precomputation can be applied in order to enhance the performance of the filling operation by avoiding the linear function evaluations that are necessary when using the method of Chapter 3.

Chapter 5 shows how the MIMD transputer network of the Disputer can be used in conjunction with the SIMD processor array in order to further improve the performance of polygon rendering operations.

Finally, a MIMD and a novel SIMD implementation of a polygon clipping algorithm are described and contrasted in Chapter 6.

Chapter 2
Graphics on General Purpose Parallel Architectures

2.1. Introduction

All the parallel architectures described in Chapter 1 have been designed especially for the efficient execution of the rendering operation. Their use in other applications is either impossible or difficult for two reasons:

i. They were designed for a specific task and are therefore inflexible.
ii. No research effort has been directed at providing other applications on these architectures.

We do not attempt to exceed the performance of special purpose graphics architectures here. Nor indeed do we claim that a graphics system based on a general purpose parallel architecture would be more cost-effective than its special purpose counterpart when they are compared *solely* in the domain of graphics. We do however believe that the users of general purpose parallel architectures can significantly increase the returns on their investment (and correspondingly reduce the investment in graphics hardware) by using algorithms such as those presented in subsequent Chapters in order to achieve high, if not state-of-the-art, graphics performance. Furthermore, our algorithms should be suitable for certain parallel special purpose graphics architectures.

Flynn has proposed two basic models of parallel architecture, Single Instruction Multiple Data stream (SIMD) and Multiple Instruction Multiple Data stream (MIMD), based on the number of different instructions that can be executed in parallel over different data [Flyn66]. This classification is very broad but it captures the most essential difference between parallel architectures, which is whether centralised or distributed control exists. At the hardware level centralised control means that there is only one *controller* controlling all the *processing elements* (PE's) while distributed control means that each PE has its own local controller (thus making up a processor) and therefore several different instruction streams can be executed in parallel. In general, the existence of a single controller makes SIMD systems cheaper to implement.

The application domain of either model is crucially affected by its mode of control. First of all, the type of parallelism inherent in a task must be considered. In programming a MIMD system we must divide our task into subtasks that exhibit *control* parallelism in order to divide *processes* that implement the subtasks among a number of processors. On the other hand for a SIMD implementation we need to extract *data* parallelism from our task in order to divide *data items* among the PE's of our SIMD system.

Another consequence of the existence of a single controller in a SIMD system is that the PE's can not be efficiently utilised if there is a wide variance in the amount of computation that has to be performed on the data item of each PE. PE's whose data items require a small amount of computation will have to be idle while more busy PE's finish their computation. Examples of such "unbalanced" tasks from the field of graphics include the evaluation of the Mandelbrot set [Mand82] and ray tracing [Whit80]. These unbalanced tasks are more suited to a MIMD implementation, perhaps based on the *processor farm* model [May87]. The processor farm model allocates tasks to processors dynamically as soon as the processors become available.

Communication between processors can form a major part of the cost of execution of a parallel program and the different ways in which parallel machines communicate affects the choice of algorithm. In SIMD systems communication takes place synchronously for all processors just like computation. For example, all processors can receive a value from their left neighbour in one communication time. Conversely, MIMD communication is usually asynchronous and can be more varied. Tightly-coupled MIMD systems use a shared memory for communication (which usually presents a bottleneck) whereas loosely-coupled MIMD systems communicate via a communication network.

This Chapter introduces two current instances of the *bit-serial* SIMD processor array, DisArray and the DAP (see §2.2), the transputer (a MIMD system component) and its programming language Occam (see §2.4), the Disputer (a system built out of DisArray and a network of transputers, see §2.5) and planar operations (operations on objects that have been mapped onto a processor array, see §2.6). We have implemented the planar operations on DisArray.

2.2. DisArray and the DAP

SIMD *processor arrays* are probably the most widespread form of parallel processor. Processor arrays were investigated in the early days of parallel processing because of their relative simplicity (there are many PE's but only one controller). Their forerunner, the SOLOMON computer [Slot62], was followed by a host of processor arrays from various vendors. The Illiac IV, Burroughs PEPE, Goodyear Aerospace STARAN and more recently the ICL DAP, CLIP (University College, London), Burroughs BSP and MPP are representative examples of the large class of processor arrays that have been designed over the past 25 years [Hock81]. A significant number of man years have been put into the development of algorithms for processor arrays. Low level vision and matrix (array) processing are two examples of fields that have used processor arrays to achieve substantial performance gains. The result has been the recognition of processor arrays as general purpose parallel machines.

DisArray [Page83] is a 16×16 bit-serial processor array. Each DisArray PE is connected to its 4 nearest neighbours (North, South, East and West) and it has toroidal (wrap-around) connections at the edges of the PE array. A number of 16-bit registers provide row and column inputs to the PE array, while each column of PE's is connected to a common column output line via open collector gates. This arrangement is shown in figure 2.1 for a 2×2 DisArray.

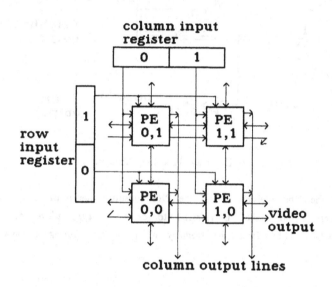

Figure 2.1. A 2×2 DisArray

A PE consists of a 256K×1 bit local memory, two 1-bit registers, an 8:1 multiplexor ALU, a 4:1 multiplexor for the selection of one of the 4 nearest neighbour outputs and a 1-bit shift register which is part of a 256-bit video shift register. The 256-bit video shift register is threaded through the 256 PE's and is used for video refresh. This is shown in figure 2.2.

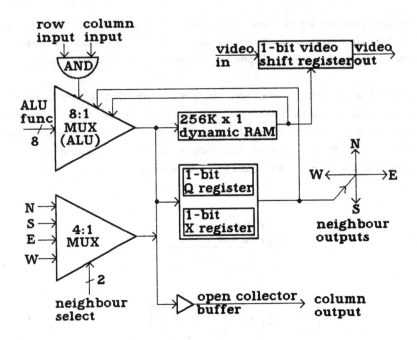

Figure 2.2. DisArray Processing Element

The collection of the 1-bit registers of all the PE's constitute the *planar* registers **Q** and **X** while a 1-bit deep memory slice is referred to as a *memory plane* or *bitplane*. A memory plane contains 1 bit from the memory of each PE. During a DisArray memory cycle:

i. A memory plane is read.

ii. The row and column input lines are logically ANDed to select a *quadrant*.

iii. An arbitrary Boolean function is applied between the memory plane and one of the planar registers in the selected quadrant while another arbitrary Boolean function is applied outside the selected quadrant.

iv. The result of the function in iii. is optionally written back to the memory location used in i. (Read/Modify/Write cycle) and/or latched into one of the two planar registers and/or sent to the column output lines.

The video controller autonomously transfers a memory plane to the video shift register by stealing a memory cycle. The video shift register is then asynchronously clocked out to the CRT at video speed. The mismatch between the *square* memory plane and the requirements of video refresh (long thin scan-lines) is overcome by an address staggering scheme [Page83].

DisArray can efficiently execute the powerful graphics primitive RasterOp [Newm79, Page83]. RasterOp operates on two equally-sized rectangular areas of the frame buffer; the *source* and the *destination*. It performs the operation:

$$destination := destination \; op \; source$$

for each corresponding pair of pixels in the *source* and *destination*. *op* is a Boolean function in the case of black and white images (1 bit per pixel) but useful extensions for colour pictures have been developed [Gutt86]. Notice that processor arrays are ideal for the parallel implementation of RasterOp since the same operation must be performed on a large data set (the two equally-sized rectangles of pixel data).

The ICL Distributed Array Processor (DAP) [Redd73, Park83], is another bit-serial processor array and the design of DisArray was partly inspired from the DAP. The main differences between a DAP and a DisArray PE are the following:

1. The DAP PE incorporates a 1-bit full adder and a 1-bit register especially for the storage of arithmetic carry. The DAP can thus perform *planar arithmetic* (see §2.6.3) very efficiently, while DisArray has to simulate planar arithmetic operations using its 8:1 multiplexor which can implement Boolean operations only. For example, planar addition costs 7 cycles per bitplane on DisArray while on the DAP it costs no more than 3 (§2.6.3). DisArray was originally built for the sole purpose of executing RasterOp efficiently and it is for this reason that the adder and the carry register were not included in its PE's.

2. DisArray has the video shift register threaded through its PE's for efficient video output. This facility is not present in the DAP, but the latest DAP marketed by AMT includes a fast data I/O channel.

In the design of the rendering algorithms presented in the following Chapters, we have not assumed the availability of any special purpose features in the processor array (such as the quadrant addressing mechanism available on the 8×8 display [Spro83]). We have only assumed some features that should be available on a general purpose processor array such as:

1. The registers and logic (full adder) in the PE's that are necessary in order to perform efficient planar arithmetic. (A general purpose processor must provide hardware support for arithmetic!).

2. The means to efficiently extract video output from the processor array memory (this is done using the shift register on DisArray and using the data I/O channel of

the AMT DAP). This facility could be designed so as to provide an efficient means for general I/O which is a necessity in general purpose processors (the DAP approach is such an example).

Processor arrays do not *have to* be bit-serial i.e. consist of bit-serial PE's and bit-wide memories. Indeed, if the applications justify it, processor arrays could be constructed out of bit-parallel PE's and memories. From now on we shall assume an $N{\times}N{\times}M$ processor array i.e. one that has M-bit wide PE data paths and can process all the elements of an $N{\times}N{\times}M$ sized object in parallel. We shall extend the performance figures of an efficient bit-serial processor, like the DAP, to the 3D case. In the case of planar arithmetic operations, the ripple carry propagation delay through the M bitplanes will be ignored on the grounds that it is negligible compared to the memory cycle.

If the decision on the trade-off between the word- and the bit-parallelism of a processor array is made at the system design stage, then the generality of the processor array will be reduced. However *reconfigurable* processor arrays will allow the choice between word- and bit-parallelism to be made at the system configuration, program compilation or even program execution stage. Jesshope describes how reconfigurability can be achieved by adding a 1-bit register to each PE, the reconfiguration register, which controls carry propagation through the PE [Jess84].

2.3. Mapping the Frame Buffer Onto a Processor Array

The $N{\times}N$ array of PE's that make up a processor array is usually much smaller than the $I{\times}I$ pixels of a typical image space (typical values of N are 8, 16, 32 and 64 while typical values of I are 512 and 1024). It is therefore necessary to consider how the frame buffer of such an "oversize" image is to be mapped onto the memories of the PE's.

There are two main ways of mapping an $I{\times}I{\times}fd$ frame buffer onto the memories of the $N{\times}N$ PE's [Redd88]. In *sheet mapping*, the frame buffer is interlaced between the memories of the PE's. PE (i,j):

$$(i,j) \mid i,j:0..N\text{-}1$$

stores in its local memory the colour of the pixels with coordinates:

$$(i+mN, \ j+nN) \mid m,n:0..(I/N)\text{-}1.$$

For example to distribute a 512×512 frame buffer among the memories of a 32×32 processor array using sheet mapping, we divide the frame buffer into 256 blocks of 32×32 pixels and assign one pixel of every block to the memory of the "corresponding" PE (there are 32×32 PE's and 32×32 pixels in each block). Conversely, in *crinkled mapping* the frame buffer is divided into contiguous blocks and each block is allocated to the memory of a single PE. In crinkled mapping PE (i,j) stores in its local memory the colour of pixels whose coordinates are:

$$(m,n) \mid m:i(I/N)..((i+1)(I/N))-1, \quad n:j(I/N)..((j+1)(I/N))-1.$$

To use the data of the above example, the 512×512 frame buffer would be divided into 1024 blocks of 16×16 pixels. Each block would then be assigned to the memory of the "corresponding" PE (there are 32×32 PE's and 32×32 blocks of pixels). In both mappings, each PE allocates $(fd)I^2/N^2$ bits of its local memory for the frame buffer. Figure 2.3 shows the pixels whose colour is stored in the memory of PE (0,0) for both the sheet and crinkled mappings.

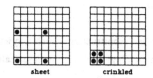

Figure 2.3. Sheet and crinkled mapping $(N=4, \ I=8)$

In general, crinkled mapping is advantageous when access to the colour of neighbouring pixels is required because communications do not have to take place. On the other hand sheet mapping is preferable when operations are performed on limited regions because it results in higher PE utilisation. Under the assumption that most of the primitives to be rendered (e.g. polygons) occupy only a small fraction of image space, sheet mapping is preferable as far as the rendering operation is concerned. DisArray uses sheet mapping and this mapping will be assumed from now on.

The processor array accesses the frame buffer in terms of *windows* ($N \times N$ square arrays of pixels called *sheets* in [Redd88]; hence the name sheet mapping). Windows are non-overlapping and aligned on boundaries that are integer multiples of N. The screen coordinates of a window are those of its bottom-left pixel, i.e. the only pixel of the window both of whose coordinates are multiples of N. The above definition of a window will be assumed in the sequel because such a window can be accessed in one cycle of the processor array (or fd cycles for an fd-bit deep frame buffer and a bit-serial processor array). If windows were aligned at arbitrary pixel boundaries, four cycles (rather than one) would be required to access them unless the processor array used the quadrant addressing scheme [Spro83].

The memory organisation of the processor array (as described above) results in a square word (the window). It turns out that the organisation of the frame buffer into square words is very advantageous in rendering operations. This is because graphical primitives such as lines and polygons are no more likely to be short and wide than tall and thin. Thus, in contrast to other memory organisations, rendering performance is not affected by the major axis of the primitive.

2.4. Occam and the Transputer

As we mentioned earlier, some tasks can not be adapted for efficient SIMD processing and the MIMD model of parallel computation may be more appropriate for these tasks. The main difference from the SIMD model is that every processor has its own controller. Until recently, there had been few practical applications of general purpose MIMD systems and pioneer MIMD systems comprised a very small number of processors. It seems that the main drawbacks of MIMD systems were:

1. The difficulty involved in constructing such systems out of off-the-shelf components and in particular providing efficient communication between processors.

2. The lack of a practical language in which to express the concepts involved in programming a MIMD system.

The advent of the transputer [INMO86] and its programming language Occam [INMO84, INMO87] provide a very promising solution to the above two problems. Transputers can easily be connected together and Occam allows one to construct parallel programs with relative ease.

The transputer is a 32-bit microprocessor with on-chip local memory and 4 bidirectional bit-serial links which enable it to be connected to 4 other transputers in order to construct a loosely-coupled MIMD system. The user physically wires transputers together using their links in order to construct networks of various topologies. The topology of a transputer network is easily modifiable (it is only a matter of specifying a "configuration" and changing the physical link connections between the transputers). Pipelines, trees, arrays and other topologies can easily be constructed out of the same transputer network according to the requirements of the task at hand.

The transputer efficiently supports the concurrent programming language Occam which is derived from Hoare's Communicating Sequential Processes (CSP) [Hoar85].

An Occam program consists of a number of *processes*. Processes can be explicitly combined to run in parallel by means of the PAR statement. Concurrent processes can communicate via *channels*. A channel provides unidirectional communication between a pair of processes. Concurrent processes may be executed by one or more transputers and Occam allows the allocation of processes to transputers to be performed with ease. "Software" channels provide communication between pairs of processes running on the same transputer while physical transputer links implement the channels of processes running on different transputers.

Occam provides non-deterministic choice (the ALT construct). A number of alternative processes are specified at a particular point in the Occam code and, at run time, if more than one of these processes is ready to execute then the one to be executed is chosen among them non-deterministically. This is useful for example in the implementation of a process which is waiting for input on a number of channels. Occam processes can, of course, also be combined in the usual ways e.g. sequentially, conditionally etc.

The data types provided in Occam initially were integers and 1D arrays of integers but the Occam language has recently been extended to include reals, multidimensional arrays and records. Type conversions are *explicit* in Occam.

2.5. The Disputer

It is often the case that both the SIMD and the MIMD parallel architectures are necessary for the efficient parallel implementation of a task. This appears to be true for example in the areas of graphics and image processing. It would be desirable therefore to have a machine that comprised both the SIMD and the MIMD parallel architectures so that, depending on the kind of task at hand, one could use either the SIMD, the MIMD or both architectures. Winder has enabled us to do just that by building a transputer controller for DisArray [Wind86]. The links of the transputer controller connect the SIMD DisArray to the MIMD transputer network which is arbitrarily extensible. The whole system is called the *Disputer* (*Dis*Array-*trans*puter) [Wind87, Page88] and it allows us to investigate dual-paradigm (SIMD-MIMD) algorithms [Wind88].

An important feature of the Disputer is that it can be programmed in Occam alone. The controller of DisArray is regarded just like any other transputer in the MIMD network, the only difference being that it has access to a special kind of primitive data type: the planar data type. The controller can thus declare variables of planar data type and perform operations on them. Of course, the planar operations are executed by DisArray whose control registers are mapped into the memory of the controller.

2.6. Planar Operations

As mentioned earlier, the Disputer is totally programmable in Occam but the transputer which controls the processor array has access to a special data type, the planar data type. We have created a library of procedures which handle the various operations on the planar data types; these are called *planar operations* and are described in this section. The planar data types and their associated operations have thus been incorporated into our programming environment and provide an interface between the SIMD and the MIMD parts of the Disputer. Planar operations are executed by the processor array and they are of use in the implementation of graphics rendering operations (among others) as later Chapters will show.

There are two basic ways of mapping numbers onto the memory of a processor array such as the DAP; *horizontal* where N N-bit numbers are mapped onto a single memory plane and *vertical* where N^2 pd-bit numbers are mapped onto pd memory planes as shown in figure 2.4.

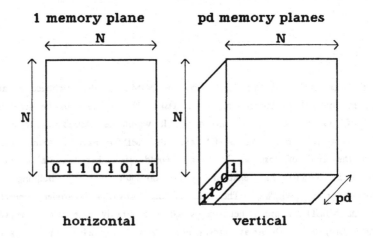

Figure 2.4. Horizontal and vertical mapping of numbers;
the bits of one number shown

We shall restrict our attention to the vertical mapping because it matches the way the frame buffer is mapped onto the processor array. Thus the bits that constitute one element (number, pixel colour) reside in the memory of a single PE.

Planar operations are performed on corresponding elements of planar objects, for all elements in parallel.

Since objects of planar data type are primitives of the processor array (in analogy to scalars being the primitive objects of a uniprocessor), we believe that the language in which the processor array is programmed should treat such objects as "first class citizens". In other words one should be able to use objects of planar data type in all the various ways that a scalar can be used; for example pass planar objects as parameters to procedures, use the basic language operators to describe operations on planar objects (rather than using procedure calls) etc. For simplicity and clarity of presentation, we shall assume that the Occam language has been extended to include planar data types and operations on them. The extensions are only defined informally here in order to simplify the description of algorithms. The planar data types of PLANAR.BOOL, PLANAR.INT and PLANAR.REAL are included as first class citizens. Thus, for example, one can declare the following primitive planar objects:

> PLANAR.INT A, B, C:
> PLANAR.BOOL P, Q, R:

rather than specify explicitly their scalar decomposition as:

> $[N][N]$ INT A, B, C:
> $[N][N]$ BOOL P, Q, R:

The above objects consist of pd and 1 memory planes of the processor array respectively. Planar integers and reals can have a number of precisions, in analogy to integers and reals; if no precision is specified in the declaration a default precision is used. We shall let pd stand for the default precision. We shall often use $[a]$ to stand for the planar object whose scalar components are defined by a.

Arrays of planar objects can be declared. For example the frame and depth buffers (FB and ZB respectively) of an $I{\times}I$-pixel image space are declared as follows:

> $[I/N,\ I/N]$ PLANAR.INT $FB,\ ZB$:

Every element of each of the above two arrays holds the portion of the frame and depth buffers that corresponds to a window of image space. We shall denote the depth of the frame and depth buffers by fd and zd respectively.

The following sections define some planar operations on the primitive planar data types of our language. If the planar data types were not primitive then the planar operations would be defined in terms of procedures with the following generic form:

```
PROC <name> (<parameters>)
    INT i,j:
    SEQ i=0 FOR N
        SEQ j=0 FOR N
            <scalar operation>
  :
```

where $<scalar\ operation>$ performs the scalar operation specified by $<name>$ between the $(i,j)^{th}$ elements of the planar objects supplied in $<parameters>$. Notice that the processor array performs all the N^2 scalar operations involved in the two nested loops in parallel.

The performance of algorithms is expressed in terms of processor array memory cycles in order to abstract away from specific technologies. Furthermore, the figures are based on the DAP design which can efficiently implement planar arithmetic operations.

The performance figures of the following sections are based on a hypothetical $N \times N \times M$ processor array which possesses sufficient planar registers and logic to perform planar operations efficiently (the DAP is a bit-serial example, i.e. $M=1$). The above declarations are assumed in the following sections.

2.6.1. Broadcast

Broadcast is a type conversion operator. It converts a scalar a into a constant planar object of the corresponding type. Each of the N^2 elements of the planar object becomes equal to a. If a is of type integer:

```
A := PLANAR.INT (a)
R := PLANAR.BOOL (TRUE)
```

are examples of broadcasts. Notice that they conform with the Occam syntax for type conversions (type conversions are explicit in Occam). Assuming that there is an M-bit wide broadcast path from the controller to the N^2 M-bit PE's, a broadcast will cost 1 array memory cycle for every M bits of the scalar being broadcast. Thus broadcasting a pd-bit scalar costs $\lceil pd/M \rceil$ cycles.

2.6.2. Planar Assignment

Planar assignment or *planar copy* is the operation of copying a planar object into another one of the same type:

$$A := B$$

The cost is 2 array cycles for every M-bitplanes; one to read an M-bit slice of B and another to write into an M-bit slice of A. The cost of a pd-bitplane planar assignment is thus $2\lceil pd/M \rceil$ array cycles.

A very useful variant of the planar assignment is the *conditional planar assignment* (called *selective* assignment by Hockney & Jesshope [Hock81]). A planar Boolean mask indicates which elements of the destination planar object are to be updated from the corresponding elements of the source:

$$A(Q) := B$$

The cost of the conditional planar assignment is $2.5\lceil pd/M \rceil$ cycles. This comprises one array cycle to read M-bitplanes of B and a Read-Modify-Write cycle to read, update and write back M-bitplanes of A.

We assume that a Read-Modify-Write cycle takes as long as 1.5 "normal" cycles. This assumption is borrowed from the DAP figures. (The Read-Modify-Write cycle will not be available on the latest DAP marketed by AMT because of constraints arising from the reduction of the cycle time from 200ns to 100ns).

2.6.3. Planar Arithmetic and Boolean Operations

The usual arithmetic and Boolean operations are provided between planar objects of the same type. Their name is derived by prefixing the word *planar* to the name of the corresponding scalar operation:

operation	cost	operation	cost
$A := B + C$	$3\{2.5\}\lceil pd/M \rceil$	$R := P \wedge Q$	$3\{2.5\}$
$A := B * C$	$2.5(pd)\lceil pd/M \rceil$	$R := \sim P$	$2\{1.5\}$

The types of the above objects are given in §2.6. The cost of each operation, in processor array memory cycles, is given along side it (the cost of the planar assignment included). The number in curly brackets should be used instead of the number to its left, if the result of the operation is one of the operands because in this case a Read-Modify-Write cycle can save part of the cost of the last (Write) cycle. Sequential code overheads, such as the loading of the addresses of planar operands, have been ignored because they are negligible compared to the cost of the array cycles of planar arithmetic operations for realistic arithmetic precisions. The sequential overheads are not negligible in the case of planar Boolean operations (where few array cycles are involved), but we shall ignore them because the cost of planar Boolean operations is small anyway and in order to simplify the task of expressing the performance of algorithms.

2.6.4. Planar Comparison

The result of a *planar comparison* between two planar integers (reals) of the same type is a planar Boolean:

$$R := A < B$$

An element of R is set to TRUE if and only if the comparison between the corresponding elements of A and B is true. The cost of a planar comparison is equal to the cost of a planar subtraction or $3\lceil pd/M \rceil$ cycles for planar integers.

2.6.5. Planar Shift

The *planar shift* allows planar integers to be shifted across word or bit boundaries. Shifting across bit boundaries, *planar bit shift*, can be done in one of two directions, to the left or to the right, and requires no communication between the PE's; the symbols $<<$ and $>>$ are used to represent left and right planar bit shifts respectively. For example the statement:

$$A := A << 2$$

has the effect of shifting each scalar element of planar integer A to the left by two bit positions. Planar bit shifting can be used to implement cheaply planar multiplications (divisions) by powers of 2. The cost of a planar bit shift will depend on whether it is implemented by actually shifting the bitplanes of the planar object or by altering the address of the first bitplane of the planar object. The latter method has no array cycle cost. The former one will cost as much as a planar copy.

Shifting across word boundaries, *planar word shift*, can be done in one of four directions; UP, DOWN, LEFT or RIGHT. For example the statement:

$$A := A \ UP \ 7$$

will shift each scalar element of A from PE (i,j) to PE $(i, (j+7) \bmod N)$. Planar word shifting involves inter-PE communication but this is cheap on a processor array because it takes place synchronously for all PE's (notice that the wrap-around connections of the processor array are used in planar word shifting). A number of "internal" processor array cycles (not memory cycles) will be used in order to perform a planar word shift on the contents of a planar register. On a processor array with the connectivity of the DAP, the number of internal cycles necessary will be equal to the number of positions shifted which will be less than or equal to $1/2N$. Internal cycles are usually much faster than memory cycles; in the case of the transputer, for example, internal cycles are 4 times faster than external memory cycles.

The DisArray implementations of a selected sample of planar operations are given in Appendix I. Notice that the number of processor array cycles in the implementations of Appendix I does not always agree with the figures given in the previous sections. This is because the DisArray PE's do not possess the registers and logic necessary for the efficient implementation of some planar operations.

2.7. Conclusion

The SIMD and MIMD parallel architectures have application domains which are largely complementary. Their integration into a single system, like the Disputer, will therefore have an application domain which is larger than that of either machine on its own. The SIMD part of the Disputer is controlled by a transputer and can thus be regarded as one of the processes of the MIMD system. The Disputer is programmable in Occam but the transputer which controls the processor array has access to a special data type, the planar data type, and planar operations are performed by the processor array. We have implemented a set of planar operations which, among other tasks, are useful for graphics as the following Chapters will show.

Chapter 3
A Parallel Incremental Rendering Method

3.1. Introduction

Incremental calculations are used where possible in raster graphics to improve the performance of algorithms by taking advantage of *coherence* i.e. the continuity of some characteristic over a part of the image. Incremental calculations maintain some memory of the previous step in the calculation and alter it by the use of an increment in order to obtain the next step.

Although it is not possible to exploit coherence by incremental computation when adjacent pixels are processed in parallel because incremental computation is based on sequential processing (memory of the previous step), it is still possible to take advantage of N-step coherence by N-step incremental calculations. This assumes that in general the area covered by a polygon spans several windows (otherwise the polygon is not N-step coherent).

In this Chapter we describe how coherence and parallelism can be exploited together in rendering. In particular we demonstrate how an $N{\times}N$ processor array that supports planar arithmetic, can efficiently evaluate a linear (or higher-order) function by using incremental calculations (N^2 of them in parallel). Thus coherence is exploited in order to improve the performance of rendering operations. In the past, the evaluation of the linear function has been used for the implementation of polygon rendering operations by Cohen [Cohe81] and Fuchs [Fuch85]. They have both proposed special purpose parallel architectures for the evaluation of the linear function. In contrast our approach uses a general purpose parallel architecture. It also has the advantage of being generalisable for the evaluation of higher-order functions. Such functions are useful in rendering as we shall see in due course.

Our method is based on the following observation: Given an $N{\times}N$ matrix R_{OLD} that contains the values of a bivariate polynomial function $F(x,y)$ at an $N{\times}N$ grid of equally spaced points (window), we can use an $N{\times}N$ processor array to compute a matrix R_{NEW} representing the values of F at a (horizontally or vertically) adjacent $N{\times}N$ grid of points by only performing d planar additions; where d is the degree of F in the relevant variable (x if the two grids are horizontal neighbours, y if they are vertical neighbours). This is, of course, the method of differences adapted for array processing.

3.2. Incremental Filling on a Processor Array

In this section we describe how a processor array can fill convex polygons using the method of differences to incrementally compute the values of a linear function within a window, from the values of the function within a neighbouring window. The filling algorithm can not handle concave polygons, but separate hardware (e.g. the MIMD transputer network of the Disputer) could split concave polygons into convex ones before passing them to the processor array for rendering; we shall not be concerned with the problem of splitting concave polygons here. For the rest of this Chapter, polygon will refer to a convex polygon.

3.2.1. Incremental Polygon Filling Algorithm

A convex n-sided polygon can be regarded as the intersection of n halfplanes defined by its n sides (including the sides themselves) or, alternatively, as the convex hull of its n vertices. The filling algorithm can be divided into two parts:

1. Determine the *extent* of the polygon, that is the smallest possible rectangle of windows that encloses the polygon (figure 3.1).

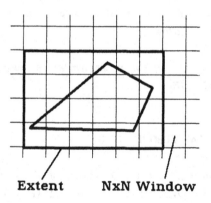

Extent   NxN Window

Figure 3.1. Extent of a polygon

2. For each window of the extent, find the intersection of the n halfplanes within the window. This identifies the pixels of the window that are actually covered by the polygon. The result is an $N{\times}N$ planar Boolean, $COVER.MASK$, which identifies the pixels of the window covered by the polygon.

The determination of the polygon's extent requires no more than 4 comparisons and 2 assignments per vertex and can be performed within the same loop as the calculation of the linear coefficients of the edges (see below). We shall now describe how to find the intersection of the n halfplanes within each window of the extent.

Side i of the polygon lies on a line with equation:

$$F^i(x,y) \;=\; a_i x + b_i y + c_i = 0. \tag{3.1}$$

The line defined by equation (3.1) divides the plane of the polygon into two halfplanes. If we compute the coefficients of the F^i by considering successive pairs of polygon vertices in an anticlockwise traversal around the polygon and the coefficients of the line equation of the edge from vertex (x_i, y_i) to (x_{i+1}, y_{i+1}) are computed as $a_i = y_i - y_{i+1}$, $b_i = x_{i+1} - x_i$ and $c_i = x_i y_{i+1} - x_{i+1} y_i$, then the polygon will always lie on the non-negative halfplane of the F^i.

For each window in the extent of the polygon we compute n planar integers R_i that contain the values of each of the n F^i functions, defined by each of the n edges of the polygon within the window (we use the terms polygon edge and polygon side as synonymous). From the planar integers R_i we derive the *COVER.MASK* for the window, which identifies the pixels of the window that are actually covered by the polygon. *COVER.MASK* is simply the Boolean ANDing of the sign planes of the n planar integers R_i for a window (where the sign plane is taken to be a planar Boolean). The Occam derivation of the *COVER.MASK* follows:

```
[n] PLANAR.INT R:              -- n is the number of polygon sides
PLANAR.BOOL COVER.MASK:

    . .

SEQ
    COVER.MASK := PLANAR.BOOL (TRUE)
    SEQ i = 0 FOR n
        ...evaluate Fi into R[i] for the coordinates of the current window
        COVER.MASK := COVER.MASK ∧ (R[i] ≥ (PLANAR.INT (0)))
```

3.2.2. Efficient Evaluation of the Linear Function on a Processor Array

Evaluating each linear function F^i for every pixel is computationally expensive; it requires 2 multiplications and 2 additions per pixel. However we can compute its values incrementally from window to window with only 1 planar addition per window (i.e. N^2 pixels) since F^i is linear. Given the planar integer R_i that contains the values of F^i at the current window, we can evaluate F^i for the horizontal successor of the current window by adding to R_i the constant planar integer H_i containing the *first forward differences* of F^i for an N-step change in x:

$$\Delta F^i_{k,\kappa} = F^i_{k+1,\kappa} - F^i_{k,\kappa}$$
$$= F^i(x+(k+1)N,y) - F^i(x+kN,y)$$
$$= (a_i(x+(k+1)N) + b_i y + c_i) - (a_i(x+kN) + b_i y + c_i)$$
$$= a_i N.$$

where $F^i_{k,\kappa} = F^i(x+kN,y)$.

In a similar manner we can compute the values of F^i for the vertical successor of the current window by adding to R_i the constant planar integer V_i of the first forward differences of F^i for an N-step change in y:

$$\Delta F^i_{\kappa,k} = F^i_{\kappa,k+1} - F^i_{\kappa,k}$$
$$= b_i N$$

having defined $F^i_{\kappa,k} = F^i(x,y+kN)$. Thus the pair of constant planar integers:

$$H_i = [a_i N] \qquad \text{and} \qquad V_i = [b_i N]$$

can be used to incrementally compute (with one planar addition) the values of F^i from window to window as shown in figure 3.2 (for a 2×2 array):

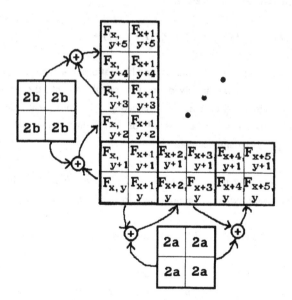

Figure 3.2. Incremental window calculations for $N=2$

For an n-sided polygon we need n planar integers R_i, n horizontal increments H_i and n vertical increments V_i. To step from one window to its (vertical or horizontal) successor we need to perform n planar additions (of the vertical or horizontal increments to the R_i) and then AND together the sign planes of the planar integers R_i to derive the COVER.MASK for the window. If the height of the average polygon of the application spans several windows, performance can be enhanced by the use of an Active Edge Table as in sequential polygon filling.

Each initial planar integer R_i can be derived by evaluating function (3.1) within the first window using planar arithmetic. Take the (precomputed) planar integers X and Y defined as:

$$X(i,j) = i \qquad Y(i,j) = j.$$

Create constant planar integers $Xoff$ and $Yoff$ (off for offset) containing the x and y coordinates of the initial window respectively. If the bottom-left pixel of the window has coordinates (xw, yw) then $Xoff$ and $Yoff$ can be defined as:

$$Xoff\ (i,j) = xw \qquad Yoff\ (i,j) = yw.$$

Adding $Xoff$ ($Yoff$) to X (Y) gives the planar integers that contain the x (y) coordinates of all pixels in the first window. Now create constant planar integers A_i, B_i and C_i each containing the value of one of the coefficients of equation (3.1) in every component. The initial planar integer R_i can be computed as:

$$R_i = A_i * (X + Xoff) + B_i * (Y + Yoff) + C_i.$$

The above computation requires 2 planar multiplications, 4 planar additions and 5 broadcasts. The two multiplications involved in the calculation of the initial R_i mean that this calculation will dominate the cost of rendering polygons that only span a few windows and we shall next describe a method of evaluating the initial planar integer R_i that does not involve planar multiplications.

The value of the function $F^i(x,y) = a_i x + b_i y + c_i$ at a pixel (point) within a window (2D discrete grid of points) whose window coordinates are (xw, yw) can be expressed as:

$$F^i(xw+x, yw+y) = F^i(xw, yw) + a_i x + b_i y$$

where (x, y) are the coordinates of the pixel relative to the window coordinates $(x, y: 0..N-1)$. Consider the evaluation of the $a_i x$ component. The multiplication of a_i by x can be replaced by a maximum of $\lceil \log_2 x \rceil$ additions of multiples of a_i and a power of 2. Such multiples of a_i can be obtained cheaply using shifts. For example to get a_i*13 we have to add a_i*2^3, a_i*2^2 and a_i.

The value of the $a_i x$ component will be the same for all points that belong to the same column of the grid. However different columns will require the summation of different multiples of a_i and powers of 2. It is therefore necessary to use conditional planar assignment (see Chapter 2).

For a grid of size $N \times N$, $\log_2 N$ planar additions with conditional planar assignment will be required for the evaluation of all the $a_i x$ components (assuming N to be a power of 2). The kth planar addition, $k:0..(\log_2 N - 1)$, will add the constant planar integer $[a_i * 2^k]$ under a planar Boolean mask which has $N/2$ columns set to TRUE and is organised as alternating groups of 2^k columns with the same value TRUE (FALSE), the leftmost group of columns being FALSE (not set). The masks for the evaluation of $a_i x$ are shown in figure 3.3 for $N=8$. The value of the constant planar integer that is added to the sum under each mask is indicated underneath the mask. Three masks are required since three planar additions are performed ($\log_2 8 = 3$).

0	1	0	1	0	1	0	1
0	1	0	1	0	1	0	1
0	1	0	1	0	1	0	1
0	1	0	1	0	1	0	1
0	1	0	1	0	1	0	1
0	1	0	1	0	1	0	1
0	1	0	1	0	1	0	1
0	1	0	1	0	1	0	1

$[a_i * 2^0]$

0	0	1	1	0	0	1	1
0	0	1	1	0	0	1	1
0	0	1	1	0	0	1	1
0	0	1	1	0	0	1	1
0	0	1	1	0	0	1	1
0	0	1	1	0	0	1	1
0	0	1	1	0	0	1	1
0	0	1	1	0	0	1	1

$[a_i * 2^1]$

0	0	0	0	1	1	1	1
0	0	0	0	1	1	1	1
0	0	0	0	1	1	1	1
0	0	0	0	1	1	1	1
0	0	0	0	1	1	1	1
0	0	0	0	1	1	1	1
0	0	0	0	1	1	1	1
0	0	0	0	1	1	1	1

$[a_i * 2^2]$

(0=FALSE, 1=TRUE)

Figure 3.3. Masks for the evaluation of $a_i x$ over an 8×8 grid

The evaluation of $b_i y$ can be carried out in a similar manner. The masks required will be equivalent to the masks used for $a_i x$ rotated by 90° anticlockwise.

The strategy for the initial evaluation of the function $F^i(x,y) = a_i x + b_i y + c_i$ over the initial window whose coordinates are (xw, yw) is then the following: the controller (or a co-processor) evaluates $F^i(xw, yw)$ and broadcasts this value to the array forming a planar integer R_i. The appropriate multiples of a_i and b_i by powers of 2 are then conditionally added to R_i as described above.

The initial evaluation of a linear function F^i is described in Occam below. We shall assume that the required planar Boolean masks (figure 3.3) have been precomputed. The masks needed for the evaluation of the $a_i x$ component are stored in an array of $\log_2 N$ planar Booleans, *V.LOG.MASK*, and those required for the $b_i y$ component in *H.LOG.MASK*:

```
--assume previous declarations
VAL log2N IS
[n] INT a, b, c:
INT xw, yw:   --the coordinates of the initial window
[n] PLANAR.INT A, B:
[log2N] PLANAR.BOOL V.LOG.MASK, H.LOG.MASK:
    . .
--Evaluation of linear function for iᵗʰ edge
SEQ
    A[i] := PLANAR.INT (a[i])
    B[i] := PLANAR.INT (b[i])
    R[i] := PLANAR.INT (((a[i] * xw) + (b[i] * yw)) + c[i])
    SEQ j = 0 FOR log2N
        SEQ
            R[i] (V.LOG.MASK[j]) := R[i] + A[i]
            R[i] (H.LOG.MASK[j]) := R[i] + B[i]
            A[i] := A[i] << 1
            B[i] := B[i] << 1
```

If we ignore the cost of the evaluation performed in the controller (which can be done in a co-processor), the cost of evaluating the function over the initial window is $2\log_2 N$ planar additions plus 3 broadcasts (of the a_i, b_i and $(a_i * xw + b_i * yw + c_i)$ values). The cost of the planar assignments is included in the cost of the operation on the rhs. The planar bit shifts can be done for free on a bit-serial processor array and very cheaply on a bit-parallel processor array, so we shall ignore their cost. A planar addition costs $2.5 * \lceil pd/M \rceil$ array cycles while a broadcast costs $\lceil pd/M \rceil$ cycles. The direct evaluation of the function (using planar multiplications) had a cost of 2 planar multiplications, 4 planar additions and 5 broadcasts. The cost of a planar multiplication is $2.5 * (pd)\lceil pd/M \rceil$ array cycles. Thus the latter method should outperform the former method (that uses multiplications) provided that:

$$5\log_2 N \lceil pd/M \rceil + 3 \lceil pd/M \rceil \; < \; 5 (pd)\lceil pd/M \rceil + 10\lceil pd/M \rceil + 5 \lceil pd/M \rceil$$

$$\text{or} \quad pd > \log_2 N - 2.4$$

which holds true in the case of the DAP ($N=32$) for $pd \geq 3$ bitplanes.

3.2.3. Accuracy of Representation

We shall now derive the accuracy (depth) of the planar arithmetic representation, pd, required in order to evaluate a linear function correctly. Given an $I{\times}I$-pixel image space, the coefficients a, b, c of the line passing through the image space points (x_i, y_i) and (x_{i+1}, y_{i+1}) are defined as:

$$a = (y_i - y_{i+1})$$
$$b = (x_{i+1} - x_i)$$
$$c = (x_i y_{i+1} - x_{i+1} y_i).$$

Since x_i, y_i, x_{i+1} and y_{i+1} can independently range between 0 and I-1, the ranges of a, b and c are:

$$-(I-1) \leq a \leq (I-1)$$
$$-(I-1) \leq b \leq (I-1)$$
$$-(I-1)^2 \leq c \leq (I-1)^2.$$

If $I = 2^Q$ then:

$\quad a$ requires a $Q+1$ bit representation

$\quad b \quad " \qquad Q+1 \quad " \qquad "$

$\quad c \quad " \qquad 2Q+1 \quad " \qquad ".$

Hence $F = ax + by + c$ will require an $r = 2Q+4$ bit representation since x and y are image space pixels requiring Q bits each. We have thus derived the number of bits required for the representation of the range of values of the linear function. One must also take into account the errors that may be introduced during the evaluation of the linear function (the initial evaluation within the first window and the subsequent incremental evaluations). If the linear function is to be evaluated over w windows, then the number of planar additions required for the evaluation is $2\log_2 N + w - 1$ (w may be the number of windows in the extent or the number of "relevant windows", see §3.2.4). Therefore the number of extra bits required in order to maintain the evaluation accurate to r bits is $\lfloor \log_2(2\log_2 N + w - 1) \rfloor + 1$. Thus the planar arithmetic representation should be: $pd = r + \lfloor \log_2(2\log_2 N + w - 1) \rfloor + 1$ bits deep. For example, if $I = 512$, $N = 32$ and $w = 4$ then $r = 22$ and a $pd = 22 + \lfloor \log_2(2\log_2 32 + 4 - 1) \rfloor + 1 = 26$ bit representation is required.

3.2.4. Visiting Only Intersecting Windows

Some windows within the extent of the polygon may not be intersected by the polygon as shown in figure 3.1. The windows that are either partially or totally covered by the polygon are called *relevant windows* (RW's), see figure 4.6. We shall now describe a method of avoiding the calculation of *COVER.MASK*'s for those windows of the extent that are not RW's. The method is applicable to convex polygons that occupy an 8-connected region i.e. a region in which any pixel can be reached from any other by a sequence of any of the eight one-pixel vertical, horizontal or diagonal moves.

Given the *COVER.MASK* for a particular RW, it is usually possible to decide whether its neighbouring windows are RW's by inspecting the appropriate boundary of the *COVER.MASK* (see figure 3.4). For example if the left boundary of the *COVER.MASK* for a window does not contain any TRUE elements then the left neighbour of that window can not be an RW. Conversely if the left boundary contains at least one TRUE element then there is a possibility that the left neighbour is an RW (although this is not certain because the polygon may not extend beyond the left boundary of the current RW). Notice that the above test does not guarantee that a neighbouring window *is* an RW; rather it can only guarantee that a neighbour *is not* an RW.

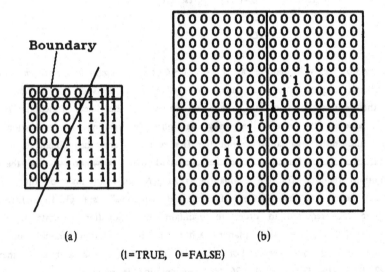

(a)   (b)

(1=TRUE, 0=FALSE)

Figure 3.4. (a) The *COVER.MASK* helps detect neighbouring RW's and
(b) A pathological 8-connected case

Let $(min.x, \ min.y)$ and $(max.x, \ max.y)$ stand for the polygon vertices with the minimum and maximum y coordinates respectively. The RW's are processed one row at a time starting from the row that contains $(min.x, \ min.y)$ and finishing at the row that contains $(max.x, \ max.y)$. Processing of a row of RW's starts at the "initial" RW for that row. The initial RW of the first row is the window that contains $(min.x, \ min.y)$. The RW's to the left of the initial RW are then processed (processing stops when the left boundary of the $COVER.MASK$ for an RW does not contain any TRUE elements). Notice that in order to incrementally calculate the values of linear function F^i for the left neighbour of a window we subtract, rather than add, the horizontal increment H_i. The RW's to the right of the initial window are processed in a similar manner.

If the polygon extends above the current row of windows then the planar integers R_i of any one RW of the row whose $COVER.MASK$ contains at least one TRUE element in its top boundary are saved because the top neighbour of that RW will be the initial window of the above row. Processing of the next row of windows starts by adding the V_i increments to the saved planar integers R_i in order to derive the R_i's, and hence the $COVER.MASK$, of the initial window of the next row. Notice that owing to the fact that the region is 8-connected, the initial window of a row (excluding the first row) may not be an RW, see the pathological case of figure 3.4. If this is the case, i.e. the $COVER.MASK$ of the initial window of a row contains no TRUE elements, then the neighbour of the initial window in the direction of $max.x$ must be visited next.

3.2.5. Processor Utilisation in Linear Function Evaluation

In this section we shall work out how well the N^2 PE's of the processor array are utilised during the evaluation of the linear function by the method described in §3.2.2 where the initial evaluation is carried out using planar additions with conditional planar assignments. For this purpose we shall define the *speedup* that a parallel processor offers over a uniprocessor (with the same bit-parallelism) as:

$$speedup = \text{(execution time on uniprocessor) /}$$
$$\text{(execution time on parallel processor)}$$

For a parallel processor with N^2 processors (or PE's) the value of the *speedup* will range between 1 and N^2. The *processor utilisation* (pu) can then be defined as:

$$pu = speedup \ / \ N^2$$

for a parallel processor with N^2 processors (or PE's) and the value of pu will range between $1/N^2$ and 1. The processor utilisation can alternatively be defined as the fraction of time that a parallel processor is engaged in useful computation but this definition does not take into account the complexity of the particular algorithm used. For a better discussion of performance metrics see §6.2.

Let us assume that a linear function is to be evaluated over an area of p adjacent pixels (which may represent the area of a polygon). For convenience we shall also assume that the p pixels occupy a square of side $\sqrt{p}$. Given the value of the linear function at a particular pixel, a uniprocessor can incrementally evaluate the linear function over the remaining $p-1$ pixels at a cost of $p-1$ additions.

In order to work out the cost involved in evaluating the linear function using the $N \times N$ processor array, we need to know how many windows are on average intersected by the square of p pixels. Since the square may be arbitrarily positioned in image space, it will on average intersect $\sqrt{p}/N+1$ rows of windows and an equivalent number of columns. That makes $(\sqrt{p}/N+1)^2$ windows. The number of planar additions required in order to evaluate the linear function over the $(\sqrt{p}/N+1)^2$ windows is then $2\log_2 N + (\sqrt{p}/N+1)^2 - 1$ as shown in §3.2.2, hence the speedup is:

$$speedup = (p-1) \; / \; (2\log_2 N + p/N^2 + 2\sqrt{p}/N)$$

(assuming that the bit-parallelism of the uniprocessor is the same as that of the processor array). The processor utilisation is thus:

$$pu = speedup \; / \; N^2$$
$$= (p-1) \; / \; (2N^2\log_2 N + p + 2N\sqrt{p}).$$

The following graph plots the processor utilisation against the number of pixels p for $N=8$, 16, 32 and 64.

Graph 3.1. Processor utilisation (pu)

versus Number of pixels (p)

(Linear Function Evaluation)

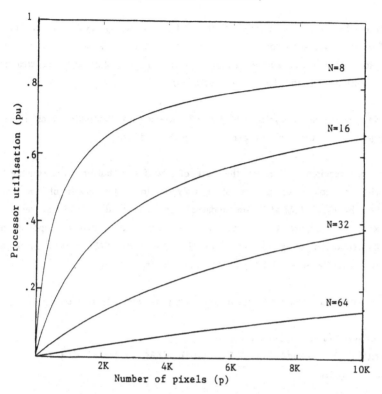

3.2.6. Performance

The rendering operations described in this Chapter can be implemented on an $N{\times}N{\times}M$ SIMD processor array. This kind of parallel processor is described in Chapter 2.

Having implemented the optimisation required to avoid visiting non-intersecting windows, the performance of our filling algorithm will depend on the number of relevant windows, w, the number of edges in the polygon, n, the depth of the planar arithmetic representation, pd, the depth of the frame buffer, fd, and the word and bit parallelism of the processor array, (N,M). Define:

t_{BROAD} to be the time needed to broadcast a scalar number to the processor array in order to create a constant pd-bit deep planar integer, i.e. a planar integer whose elements are all equal to the scalar. $t_{BROAD} = \lceil pd/M \rceil$ array cycles (§2.6.1).

t_{ADD} to be the time required to perform an $N \times N \times (pd)$ planar addition, with the result planar integer being one of the operands, using an $N \times N \times M$ processor array. $t_{ADD} = 2.5 * \lceil pd/M \rceil$ array cycles (§2.6.3).

$t_{EVAL} = 2\log_2 N * t_{ADD} + 5 * t_{BROAD} = 5\log_2 N * \lceil pd/M \rceil + 5 * \lceil pd/M \rceil$ array cycles to be the time required for the evaluation of the first planar integer R_i ($2\log_2 N$ planar additions plus 3 broadcasts of a_i, b_i and $F^i(xw,yw)$ as shown in §3.2.2) and the creation of the 2 increments $[a_i N]$ and $[b_i N]$ (2 broadcasts).

$t_{INC} = t_{ADD} = 2.5 * \lceil pd/M \rceil$ array cycles, the cost of incrementally computing each subsequent planar integer R_i i.e. the time to perform a planar addition.

$t_{F.UPDATE}$ as the time required to update the part of the frame buffer corresponding to a window with the colour or texture of a polygon (only the pixels of the window indicated by the COVER.MASK are updated). In general, the colour or texture has to be conditionally assigned to the part of the frame buffer that corresponds to the window, the condition being the value of the COVER.MASK at each pixel within the window. Thus $t_{F.UPDATE} = 2.5 * \lceil fd/M \rceil$ array cycles.

The time required to fill an n-sided polygon intersecting w windows is then:

$$T_{FILL} = n\, t_{EVAL} + (w-1)n\, t_{INC} + w\, t_{F.UPDATE}$$
$$= n((5\log_2 N + 5) * \lceil pd/M \rceil) + 2.5 * n * (w-1)\lceil pd/M \rceil + 2.5 * w * \lceil fd/M \rceil$$

array cycles.

The term $n\, t_{EVAL}$ represents the initialisation time i.e. the time to compute the first planar integers R_i and the increments for the linear function of each of the n edges of the polygon. $(w-1)n\, t_{INC}$ is the time taken to incrementally compute the rest of the planar integers R_i (we compute n planar inegers R_i for each relevant window). We have chosen to ignore the time it takes to AND the sign planes of the planar integers R_i as this will be negligible compared to the n planar additions performed in the incremental calculation of the planar integers R_i for each window. $w\, t_{F.UPDATE}$ is the cost of updating the part of the frame buffer that corresponds to each of the w relevant windows with the polygon's colour. The COVER.MASK indicates which pixels of each window to update and its derivation is described in §3.2.1.

We shall now estimate the number of processor array cycles involved in the evaluation of a linear function, i.e. in t_{EVAL} and t_{INC}, on two example processor arrays that can perform planar arithmetic with reasonable efficiency (such as the DAP). We shall consider the cases of a bit-serial and a bit-parallel processor array. The sequential code overheads of planar arithmetic operations are negligible.

Let us assume that the processor array is a 32×32 bit-serial DAP (N=32, M=1), and that the planar integers are 32 bits deep (pd=32). A broadcast then takes 32 cycles (t_{BROAD}=32) while a planar addition takes $2.5 * 32 = 80$ cycles (t_{ADD}=80) provided the result is one of the operands which is our case. The number of processor array cycles in t_{EVAL} and t_{INC} is then:

	Array Cycles	(32×32 processor array)
t_{EVAL}	$5\log_2 N * \lceil pd/M \rceil + 5 * \lceil pd/M \rceil$	960
t_{INC}	$2.5 \lceil pd/M \rceil$	80

for the evaluation of the linear function to 32 bits of accuracy over a 32×32 grid.

If a cubic processor array were available, say 8×8×16 (=1024) i.e. (N=8, M=16) for comparison with the 32×32 (=1024) bit-serial processor array, then planar arithmetic could be performed 16-bit-parallel. A broadcast would cost $t_{BROAD} = \lceil 32/16 \rceil = 2$ array cycles because 16 bitplanes of the planar number would be created in parallel. The cost of t_{EVAL} and t_{INC} would then be:

	Array Cycles	(8×8×16 processor array)
t_{EVAL}	$5\log_2 N * \lceil pd/M \rceil + 5 * \lceil pd/M \rceil$	40
t_{INC}	$2.5 \lceil pd/M \rceil$	5

for the evaluation of the linear function to 32 bits of accuracy over an 8×8 grid.

Evaluating the linear function over a 32×32 grid, i.e. 16 8×8 grids, using the 8×8×16 processor array would therefore cost 40 + (15 * 5) = 115 cycles which is far shorter than the 960 cycles required by the 32×32 bit-serial processor array.

3.2.7. Word- versus Bit-Parallelism

It is interesting to understand why the above difference arises between the performances of the above two processor arrays which use the same amount of silicon. Both processor arrays can perform the incremental evaluation of the linear function equally efficiently (the 32×32 processor array takes 80 cycles to incrementally evaluate the linear function over a 32×32 grid, and the 8×8×16 processor array also requires 16*5 = 80 cycles for the incremental evaluation of the linear function over the same grid). The difference between the performances of the two processor arrays in evaluating the linear function must therefore result from differences in the cost of the initial evaluation i.e. the t_{EVAL} times. The ratio of the t_{EVAL} times of the two processor arrays, $r1 = 960/40$, is not equal to the ratio of their areas, $r2 = 32^2/8^2$. (In contrast the ratio of the t_{INC} times, $80/5$, is equal to the ratio of their areas). The disparity between $r1$ and $r2$ arises because the amount of computation involved in t_{EVAL} is proportional to the area of the grid times the log of the grid's side. If we ignore the cost of the broadcasts involved in t_{EVAL}, then the amount of computation required for the initial evaluation of a linear function over an $N{\times}N$ grid is $2\log_2 N$ planar additions or $N^2 2\log_2 N$ additions. Thus the computation cost per grid point is proportional to $N^2 2\log_2 N / N^2$ or $2\log_2 N$ i.e. it is proportional to the logarithm of the side of the grid (the processor utilisation decreases as N increases, §3.2.5). Therefore the smaller the area of the grid, the more efficient the initial evaluation of the linear function will be. It is thus advantageous to use the available silicon in giving the processor array greater depth (bit-parallelism) rather than greater area (word-parallelism) as far as the evaluation of the linear function is concerned.

Clearly the larger we make N and M the better the performance (provided the extra parallelism can be utilised in some cases). But we must also take cost-effectiveness into account; the area of the processor array should therefore be commensurate with the average polygon size and its bit-parallelism should be commensurate with the required planar arithmetic accuracy (the planar arithmetic accuracy, pd, is also dependent on the average polygon size, see §3.2.3). However the average polygon size is highly application dependent.

Reconfigurable processor arrays (see §2.2) will allow the decision on the trade-off between word- and bit-parallelism to be postponed until the system configuration, program compilation or even program execution stage, thus avoiding the restriction in generality imposed by making the above decision at the system design stage.

3.3. Incremental Hidden Surface Elimination on a Processor Array

The calculations for hidden surface elimination (HSE) using the z-buffer algorithm and smooth shading (SS) for planar polygons using the Gouraud method (see §3.4.2) are both based on linear interpolations. HSE varies the z variable of a plane in XYZ space while SS varies the r,g and b variables of three planes in XYR, XYG and XYB spaces respectively (R,G and B standing for the Red, Green and Blue colour components). The solution to one of the two problems implies a solution to the other.

The perspective transformation that maps the vertices of a polygon from eye to image space is chosen so that an eye space plane is transformed into an image space plane [Newm79]. Thus the image space coordinates of a polygon will lie on a plane with equation:

$$a\,x + by + cz + d = 0 \qquad (3.2)$$

which can be expressed as a linear function of x and y when solved for z:

$$Z(x,y) \;=\; Ax \;+\; By \;+\; C \qquad (3.3)$$

where $A = -a/c$, $B = -b/c$ and $C = -d/c$. Given the coordinates of a pixel (x,y), function (3.3) produces the depth (z) of the polygon's plane at that pixel. The z value required for HSE (z-buffer algorithm) can therefore be computed incrementally on a processor array in a manner similar to the calculation of function (3.1) for filling. A planar integer D with the values of function (3.3) within the first window intersected by the polygon is calculated at a cost of $2\log_2 N$ planar additions. The planar integers D for subsequent relevant windows are computed incrementally at a cost of 1 planar addition each. The horizontal and vertical increments for function (3.3) are $[-N(a/c)]$ and $[-N(b/c)]$ respectively.

Arithmetic overflow in the calculation of the planar integer D can be avoided if hither and yon clipping is performed. Hither and yon clipping restricts all z_e coordinates (in the eye coordinate system) to be in the range:

$$z_{\text{HITHER}} \;\leq\; z_e \;\leq\; z_{\text{YON}}.$$

The perspective transformation then maps this range onto a new range that fully utilises the zd bits of the z-buffer. Assuming the definitions of §3.2.6, the time required to compute the planar integers D for an n-sided polygon which has w relevant windows is $t_{\text{EVAL}} + (w-1)\,t_{\text{INC}}$. The z-buffer HSE algorithm also requires one planar comparison and one conditional planar assignment per window (between the part of the z-buffer that corresponds to the window and the planar integer D for the same window, see §3.5). Define:

$t_{\text{ZUPDATE}} = 2.5\lceil zd/M\rceil$ to be the time required to update the z-buffer by one conditional planar assignment.

$t_{\text{COMP}} = 3\lceil pd/M\rceil$ to be the cost of a planar comparison.

The cost of performing the z-buffer algorithm on a polygon which has w relevant windows is:

$$
\begin{aligned}
T_{\text{HSE}} \;=\;& t_{\text{EVAL}} + (w-1)\,t_{\text{INC}} + w\,(t_{\text{ZUPDATE}} + t_{\text{COMP}}) \\
=\;& (5\log_2 N\lceil pd/M\rceil + 5\lceil pd/M\rceil) + (w-1)\,2.5\lceil pd/M\rceil \\
& + w\,(2.5\lceil zd/M\rceil + 3\lceil pd/M\rceil).
\end{aligned}
$$

3.4. Texturing and Shading

Once the *COVER.MASK* for a particular window has been calculated, there is a choice of techniques for shading the pixels of the window indicated by the *COVER.MASK*. If *COVER.MASK* is combined with an fd-bit planar integer S whose scalar components contain the same colour value, then flat shading is achieved. Texture mapping and smooth shading can be implemented by storing in S a texture map or interpolated intensity values respectively as shown in the following two subsections.

3.4.1. Texture Mapping

An $N{\times}N$ texture map can be replicated within a polygon at very little cost additional to filling the polygon with a constant colour. Instead of logically combining the *COVER.MASK* for a window with an fd-bit planar integer which represents a colour, we can combine it with an fd-bit planar integer which represents a texture map (figure 3.5).

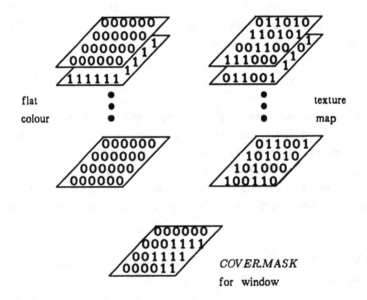

Figure 3.5. Colour versus texture

Texture maps with an arbitrary reference point and an arbitrary size are often desirable. An arbitrary reference point (rx, ry) can be accomodated by performing the following planar word shifts on the planar integer representing the texture map before it is used:

UP $(ry \mod N)$ and

RIGHT $(rx \mod N)$

To provide texture maps of arbitrary size we can use RasterOp to replicate a smaller texture map appropriately in order to create an $N \times N$ sized texture map or pick the appropriate $N \times N$ part of a larger texture map or a combination of the two, for each window we visit. Texture maps whose height and width are multiples or factors of N can be provided more efficiently by:

- using alternate sub-regions of the texture map if both its height and width are multiples of N (figure 3.6a),
- replicating the texture map (once) to create an $N \times N$ texture map if its height and width are factors of N (figure 3.6b),
- a combination of the above two if one of the texture map's dimensions is a multiple and the other a factor of N.

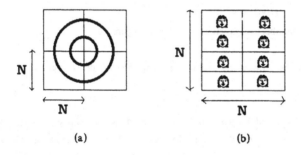

(a)   (b)

Figure 3.6. Texture maps whose size is (a) multiple or (b) factor of $N \times N$

3.4.2. Incremental Smooth Shading on a Processor Array

The linear interpolation that has to be performed in step 4 of the Gouraud shading technique (see §1.3.3) can be implemented by the evaluation of a bivariate linear function over the area of the polygon [Fuch85]. The required function is derived by calculating the plane equation through the XYC-space vertices of the polygon (where the third component, C, is the intensity calculated for each vertex) and solving that equation for C. If RGB colour is used then 3 linear functions must be evaluated; one for each of the XYR, XYG and XYB spaces. However, unless the polygon is a triangle its colour space vertices may not be co-planar. There are two possible approaches:

1. To divide the polygon until we obtain subpolygons whose colour space vertices are co-planar or we reach the triangle. This division should be performed separately for each

colour component and could be achieved, for example, by the MIMD network of the Disputer.

2. To employ an approximation technique in order to derive a plane equation that is closely related to the (non co-planar) colour space vertices of the polygon. Such a technique has been suggested by Newell and is described in [Suth74a]. Take the XYR space vertices of the polygon. The a, b and c coefficients of the XYR plane equation are determined as follows:

$$a = \Sigma \ (y_i - y_j)(r_i + r_j)$$
$$b = \Sigma \ (r_i - r_j)(x_i + x_j)$$
$$c = \Sigma \ (x_i - x_j)(y_i + y_j)$$

where

$(x_i, \ y_i, \ r_i)$ is the ith polygon vertex in XYR space
i: $0 .. n\text{-}1$
$j = (i\text{+}1$ if $i < (n\text{-}1)$ else $0)$
n is the number of vertices in the polygon.

The d coefficient can be found by using the coordinates of a vertex to solve the plane equation for d.

The bivariate linear function(s) used in smooth shading are incrementally evaluated on a processor array as shown in §3.2.2. Thus for each relevant window a planar integer S is calculated that contains the interpolated shade for each pixel within the window.

Non-planar objects can be shaded by finding the appropriate shading function over the visible area of the object and evaluating that function. Higher-order function evaluation is described in §3.7.

If the polygon is not subdivided for the purpose of shading, then the time taken to compute the planar integers S for smooth shading will be equivalent to the cost of evaluating 3 linear functions (one for each of the Red Green and Blue colour components) over the w relevant windows:

$$T_{SS} = 3 * (t_{EVAL} + (w\text{-}1) t_{INC}).$$

In the case of a grey scale display, only one linear function has to be evaluated.

3.5. Merging Fill, HSE and SS

The filling algorithm determines the planar Boolean $COVER.MASK$ for each relevant window. $COVER.MASK$ identifies the pixels of the window that the polygon covers. The HSE algorithm evaluates planar integers D that contain the depth of the pixels within each relevant window, compares D against the part of the z-buffer that corresponds to the window and updates the z-buffer where necessary. The SS algorithm evaluates planar integers S that contain the shade of the pixels within each relevant window. S may alternatively contain a constant colour (flat shading) or a texture map if smooth shading is not used. The frame buffer (FB) and z-buffer (ZB) are arrays of planar integers and consist of one planar integer for every window in image space. The ZB is used to implement the familiar z-buffer HSE algorithm described in §1.3.2. Here is how the FB and ZB are updated in Occam, once the $COVER.MASK$ and the planar integers D and S have been determined for window (xw, yw):

```
VAL I IS            --I×I image space
VAL N IS            --N×N processor array
[I/N, I/N] PLANAR.INT FB, ZB:     --assume they have the same depth
PLANAR.INT S, D:
PLANAR.BOOL COVER.MASK:
INT xw, yw:
    . .
SEQ
    COVER.MASK := COVER.MASK ∧ (D < ZB[xw, yw])
    FB[xw, yw] (COVER.MASK) := S
    ZB[xw, yw] (COVER.MASK) := D
```

Notice that it is the filling algorithm that decides which windows to visit, see §3.2.4. The performance of the combined rendering algorithm incorporating Fill, HSE and SS will be:

$$T_{FILL, HSE, SS} = T_{FILL} + T_{HSE} + T_{SS}$$
$$= (n+4)\, t_{EVAL} + ((n+4)\,(w-1))\, t_{INC} + w\,(t_{F.UPDATE} + t_{Z.UPDATE} + t_{COMP})$$

where T_{FILL}, T_{HSE} and T_{SS} were defined in §3.2.6, §3.3 and §3.4.2 respectively. If smooth shading is not used, but a flat colour or texture is used to fill the polygon, then the cost of the filling and HSE operations will be:

$$T_{FILL, HSE} = T_{FILL} + T_{HSE}$$
$$= (n+1)\, t_{EVAL} + ((n+1)\,(w-1))\, t_{INC} + w\,(t_{F.UPDATE} + t_{Z.UPDATE} + t_{COMP}).$$

Notice that the above algorithms can be used independently of each other. If, for example, we can compute the *COVER.MASK* for filling more quickly by using precomputed surface patches as described in Chapter 4, the incremental HSE and SS algorithms can still be utilised.

The rendering algorithms discussed above are similar to those used in Pixel-planes [Fuch85]. The main difference between our approach and Pixel-planes lies in the way the linear function is evaluated. Pixel-planes uses a broadcast system, the *multiplier trees*, in order to evaluate the linear function "on the fly" for the coordinates of every pixel in image space (notice that, for a typical polygon, most of these values are not useful). In contrast, our $N \times N$ processor array incrementally computes the linear function using the ALU's of its PE's for one $N \times N$ window at a time; the linear function is only evaluated within those windows that intersect the polygon.

3.6. Anti-aliasing

We shall discuss two methods of anti-aliasing polygons; both are based on extensions of the filling algorithm. The first method (§3.6.1) can be classified as pre-filtering and the second (§3.6.2) as post-filtering.

3.6.1. Anti-aliasing by Normalisation of F(x,y) = ax + by + c

One way of anti-aliasing an edge of a polygon is to normalise the coefficients of the function for that edge so that its evaluation at a particular pixel gives the distance of the centre of that pixel from the edge. For example, dividing each coefficient of $F(x,y) = ax + by + c$ by:

$$\sqrt{(a^2 + b^2)}$$

will result in a function which, given the coordinates (x,y) of a pixel, will produce the distance (in pixels) of the pixel (x,y) from the line it represents if equated to 0. Of course normalisation would be carried out by the controller of the processor array or a co-processor.

The sign of the normalised function for the coordinates of a particular pixel will be the same as that of its unnormalised counterpart and the inside/outside test remains the same. However the coordinates (x,y) of a partially covered pixel will give a value in the range $-1 < F(x,y) < 1$ to the normalised function F. Values near +1 mean that the pixel is almost totally covered by the edge of the polygon, while values near -1 mean that only a small part of the pixel is covered. These fractional values of F are mapped onto pixel intensities. Note that planar reals or planar integers with suitable scaling should be used.

The above anti-aliasing method does not work properly for pixels intersected by more than one polygon edge. This is because we have no information as to which part of a pixel is covered by each of the polygon edges in order to determine the proper intensity for the pixel. The next anti-aliasing method, pixel subdivision, provides this information.

3.6.2. Anti-aliasing by Change of Resolution

An image can be anti-aliased by performing the filling operation at a subpixel resolution (i.e. a resolution which is higher than the display resolution) and then determining the intensity of each pixel by averaging the intensities of its subpixels (post-filtering). It is particularly simple to use a processor array in order to perform the averaging (or weighted averaging) from a high resolution to a low resolution image. Page, for example, has used planar arithmetic in order to implement weighted averaging on DisArray for image processing operations [Page88]. However every subdivision of a pixel into m subpixels increases by m the number of grid points over which each polygon edge function has to be evaluated. Furthermore, many of these subpixel evaluations will be wasted for pixels that are totally covered by the polygon or are not intersected at all. Ideally, we would only like to increase the resolution for those pixels that are *partially* covered by the polygon in order to determine what portion of them is covered and hence their intensity. Since our unit picture element is the window, the nearest we can get to increasing the resolution of partially covered pixels is to increase the resolution of partially covered windows. Increasing the resolution is a matter of evaluating the function of a polygon's edge F at a subpixel grid for subwindows that are near the edge i.e. near the 0 values of F. Figure 3.7 shows how a window is subdivided into subwindows of higher resolution near the edges of a polygon.

window

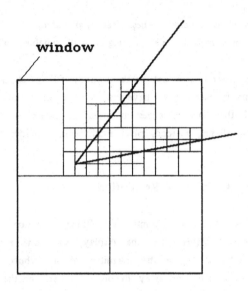

Figure 3.7. Increasing the resolution near the edges of a polygon

To increase the resolution by 1 bit within a window, the window is divided into two subwindows each of which contains as many subpixels as the original window contained pixels. This process is repeated recursively for the appropriate subwindows until the desired resolution is reached. Subdivisions are carried out depth first in some predetermined order e.g. left subwindow before right subwindow, bottom subwindow before top subwindow. Only the F functions of the relevant (intersecting) edges are carried on from one level of resolution to the next. When the maximum depth is reached, the sign planes of the F functions still relevant are ANDed together (if more than one) to determine the subwindow $COVER.MASK$. The number of TRUE elements in the part of the subwindow $COVER.MASK$ corresponding to a pixel is then counted and the intensity of the pixel is determined.

We shall now consider how a SIMD processor array can achieve the increase in resolution. Given a planar integer (or planar real) R that contains the evaluation of a linear function $F(x,y)=ax+by+c$ over an $N{\times}N$ grid that represents the pixels of a window, we want to derive a planar integer R' that contains the evaluation of F over another $N{\times}N$ grid that represents the subpixels of a subwindow of the original window. As figure 3.8 shows, R'_{LEFT}, the evaluation of F for the left subwindow of a window, can be derived from R by subtracting $ia/2$ from each element $(i,j : 0..N{-}1)$ of R.

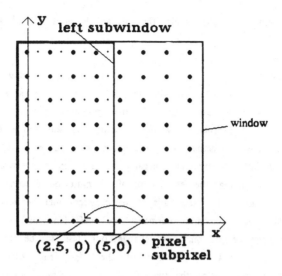

Figure 3.8. Window, subwindow, pixels and subpixels

In a similar manner the R' for the other subwindows of a window can be derived:

$$R'_{\text{LEFT}} \quad\;\; = \; R - [ia/2]$$
$$R'_{\text{RIGHT}} \quad = \; R + [(N-i)a/2]$$
$$R'_{\text{LEFT,BOTTOM}} = \; R'_{\text{LEFT}} - [jb/2]$$
$$R'_{\text{LEFT,TOP}} \;\; = \; R'_{\text{LEFT}} + [(N-j)b/2]$$

etc.

Notice that $R'_{\text{LEFT,BOTTOM}}$ and $R'_{\text{LEFT,TOP}}$ contain the evaluation of F within a "quarter-window" and are derived from R'_{LEFT} because we have assumed that the resolution is first increased horizontally and then vertically (if necessary).

Further increases in resolution are achieved in a similar manner. For example to go from subpixel to subsubpixel resolution we use the planar integers $[ia/4]$, $[(N-i)a/4]$, $[jb/4]$ and $[(N-j)b/4]$. In general to go from sub^{k}pixel to sub^{k+1}pixel resolution (where sub^{0}pixel = pixel resolution) we use the planar integers:

$$[ia/2^{k+1}], \; [(N-i)a/2^{k+1}], \; [jb/2^{k+1}] \text{ and } [(N-j)b/2^{k+1}].$$

One planar addition per edge function is required to increase the resolution by 1 bit in a particular subwindow. The planar integers that are required to facilitate the increase in resolution are computed anyway for each F function! $[ia]$ and $[jb]$ are computed as part of the evaluation of F for the first window, $[aN]$ and $[bN]$ are the horizontal and vertical window increments of F. Thus only 2 planar subtractions are required in order to derive $[(N-i)a]$ and $[(N-j)b]$ while the planar divisions by 2^k are done cheaply by planar bit shifts.

Let sub^{k}window stand for one of the 2^k subwindows of a window at resolution level k. How do we determine whether a sub^{k}window has to be subdivided into 2 higher resolution sub^{k+1}windows i.e. whether an edge of the polygon partially covers any of the sub^{k}window's pixels? The simplest way of detecting the intersection of an edge with the sub^{k}window is to check whether the evaluation of the edge function F within the sub^{k}window contains both positive and negative values. In other words the sign plane of the planar integer containing the evaluation of F must be checked for the existence of both 0's and 1's. However this test fails to detect edges that lie *between* sub^{k}windows. In order to detect such edges we must normalise the coefficients of each edge function F, as described in the previous section, and change our test to be the detection of values between 1 and -1 i.e. test the distance of the edge from each sub^{k}pixel within the sub^{k}window. With suitable scaling the use of planar reals could be avoided.

Once the highest resolution d is reached, it is necessary to count the number of sub^{d}pixels of a particular pixel that are covered by the polygon in order to determine the intensity of the pixel.

Although the anti-aliasing method just described can correctly handle multiple edges of the same polygon intersecting a pixel, it can not handle the case of multiple polygons intersecting a pixel. This is a limitation inherent in polygon serial systems that do not employ a high resolution frame buffer (the usual post-filtering technique does), because the pixel coverage information is lost between the processing of subsequent polygons. A possible solution to this problem involves the deployment of a high resolution frame buffer which can store subpixel intensities for pixels which contain fine detail. The averaging of subpixel intensities could then be performed after all polygons are rendered.

If the method of selectively increasing the resolution of the grid over which a linear function F is evaluated was used to evaluate F over *all* the subwindows of a particular window at depth d i.e. at $d+1$ times greater resolution, then $2^{d+1}-1$ planar additions would be required. This is because F is evaluated at $d+1$ different resolutions over the same window although only the highest resolution is actually used. In that case the usual post-filtering method of evaluating F at the highest resolution only over the 2^d subwindows would only require 2^d planar additions. The more complex an image is (i.e. the smaller the average polygon size), the less attractive the method of selectively increasing the resolution becomes when compared to the usual post-filtering method of computing the image at the highest resolution only.

3.7. Non-Linear Functions: Evaluation on a Processor Array and Rendering Usage

Our method of incrementally estimating the values of a function from one window to another can be applied to any polynomial function F. The theory of *successive differences* tells us that if F is a polynomial function of degree d in a particular variable then the $(d+1)^{\text{th}}$ differences of F with respect to that variable vanish i.e. $\Delta^{d+1}F = 0$. We thus need d planar integers to store the d differences (increments) of F for each of its 2 variables. To incrementally calculate the values of F at a window we must perform d planar additions. Planar addition i adds the $((d-i)+1)^{\text{th}}$ increment to the $(d-i)^{\text{th}}$ increment (the 0th increment is the planar integer containing the old values of the function).

Let us now consider the evaluation of a non-linear bivariate polynomial function within the initial window. In fact, all apart from one of the increments of a non-linear polynomial function will require the evaluation of a non-constant function and the evaluation of these increments within the initial window will have to be done in the same way. The linear increment can be evaluated more efficiently as shown in §3.2.2.

If the function does not contain $x^d y^e$ terms, then the evaluation within the initial window can be split into the evaluation of a univariate polynomial in x and the evaluation of a univariate polynomial in y. The two evaluations must then be added by a planar addition. Horner's rule allows us to evaluate a general univariate polynomial of degree d using d multiplications and d additions as follows:

$$F(x) = ((..(a_d x) + a_{d-1})x + a_{d-2})x +..+ a_1)x + a_0.$$

This technique can easily be applied to the evaluation of a univariate polynomial function at N^2 points in parallel. Having created the planar integers X and $Xoff$ (see §3.2.2) the univariate polynomial:

$$F(x) = a_d x^d + a_{d-1} x^{d-1} + .. + a_0$$

can be evaluated within the initial window as the following Occam program fragment shows:

```
INT a₀, a₁ . . a_d:
PLANAR.INT --all other variables
. .
SEQ
    XT := X + Xoff
    A_d := PLANAR.INT (a_d)
    . .
    A₀ := PLANAR.INT (a₀)
    R := (..(A_d*XT) + A_{d-1})*XT) + A_{d-2})*XT) +..+ A₁)*XT) + A₀
```

The cost of the above evaluation is d planar multiplications and d planar additions. The univariate polynomial in y is evaluated over the same square grid of points in a similar manner and then added to the planar integer R.

If the polynomial to be evaluated contains $x^d y^e$ terms, then the y^e values should be precomputed and multiplied by the constant coefficient of the $x^d y^e$ terms. The $x^d y^e$ terms are then computed during the evaluation of the univariate polynomial in x, but these terms must be ignored during the evaluation of the univariate polynomial in y.

It is interesting to see whether we can improve the performance of non-linear function evaluation within the initial window by the methods we used in order to improve the performance of linear function evaluation in §3.2.2. Firstly, there is the possibility of precomputing planar numbers containing the evaluation of x^d terms. However if x^d is not a linear term, it will not be possible to derive the evaluation of x^d within an arbitrary window by adding a planar integer containing an offset to the evaluation of x^d at the leftmost window. We would therefore need to use an amount of memory proportional to the x-dimension of image space for the storage of the planar integers containing the precomputed x^d terms. A second possibility is the implementation of each of the planar multiplications involved in Horner's rule by $\log_2 N$ planar additions. The greater the depth of the planar arithmetic, pd, the more attractive this method will be compared to the normal planar multiplications.

The evaluation of polynomial functions over a discrete grid of points (and hence the methods we have presented in §3.2.2 and §3.7 for the efficient evaluation of polynomial functions using a processor array) has a range of applications which is much wider than polygon rendering. Another possible graphics application is 3D rendering. Kaufman has described a 3D frame buffer and has generalised the sequential scan conversion algorithms to 3D objects [Kauf87]. Such a system is useful mainly for the combination of 3D images arising from sources such as CAT-scan with 3D synthetic images. The 3D synthetic images are constructed by rendering 3D geometrical objects into the 3D frame buffer. A processor array can be used to speed up the rendering of the 3D objects using a set of algorithms similar to those described in this Chapter. For example a convex polyhedron could be filled (in the 3D frame buffer) by evaluating the plane function for each of its faces in a manner similar to the filling of a convex polygon described in §3.2. Another candidate graphical application is contour plotting because contour curves are often defined by polynomial functions.

The above discussion does not claim to exhaust the subject of efficient evaluation of non-linear polynomial functions on processor arrays. The topic is deeper than it initially appeared to us and provides a stimulus for further research. The next two sections describe two rendering applications of the evaluation of non-linear functions.

3.7.1. Filling Curved Convex Areas

It is possible to fill any convex area whose boundary is (partially or totally) defined by non-linear polynomial equations; "convex" here means that the area is not entered by (the extensions of) any of the curves that define its boundary. The algorithm remains as for the convex polygon case except that for each bounding curve we must use the appropriate increments. Of course, the resulting filling algorithms will be rather inefficient due to the cost of evaluating non-linear polynomial functions and should be optimised by taking advantage of known properties of the type of the area being filled.

Let us try to determine the horizontal increments for the circle. The equation of a circle with centre (x_1, y_1) and radius R is:

$$F(x,y) = (x - x_1)^2 + (y - y_1)^2 - R^2 = 0.$$

Since F is second degree in x, its 3rd differences vanish and two increments are needed for variable x. We shall now compute the initial values of the first increment and the values of the second increment (which is constant) for N-step changes in x. The initial value of the first horizontal increment at position (x,y) is given by:

$$
\begin{aligned}
\Delta F_{0,\text{м}} &= F_{1,\text{м}} - F_{0,\text{м}} \\
&= F(x+N, y) - F(x,y) \\
&= (((x+N) - x_1)^2 + (y - y_1)^2 - R^2) - ((x - x_1)^2 + (y - y_1)^2 - R^2) \\
&= 2Nx - 2Nx_1 + N^2.
\end{aligned}
$$

where $F_{k,\text{м}} = F(x+kN, y)$. We can estimate the value of the second horizontal increment (which represents the *second differences* of F and is constant) by subtracting any two successive *first differences* of F:

$$\Delta^2 F_{k,N} = \Delta F_{k+1,N} - \Delta F_{k,N}$$
$$= (F_{k+2,N} - F_{k+1,N}) - (F_{k+1,N} - F_{k,N})$$
$$= (F(x+(k+2)N, y) - F(x+(k+1)N, y)) - (F(x+(k+1)N, y) - F(x+kN, y))$$
$$= 2N^2.$$

To incrementally calculate the planar integer that contains the values of F at a window from its evaluation at a (horizontally) neighbouring window, we add the second increment to the first one and then add the new first increment to the previous evaluation of F. This costs 2 planar additions which is what we would expect since F is of degree 2 in x.

The vertical increments for the equation of the circle could similarly be determined to be the first $(2Ny - 2Ny_1 + N^2)$ initially and the second $(2N^2)$.

3.7.2. Hidden Surface Elimination of Non-Planar Surfaces

In the same way that we extended the filling algorithm to non-linear equations in §3.7.1, we can extend the HSE algorithm for non-planar surfaces. The depth of the surface is expressed as a function Z of x and y. The number of increments required and the number of planar additions for each window will depend on the degree of x and y in Z. For a planar surface like a polygon, one increment is required for each direction and one planar addition per window. Let us now try to derive the horizontal depth increments for the sphere which can be used for HSE. The equation of a sphere with centre (x_1, y_1, z_1) and radius R:

$$(x-x_1)^2 + (y-y_1)^2 + (z-z_1)^2 = R^2$$

when solved for z becomes:

$$Z(x,y) = z_1 \pm \sqrt{(R^2 - (x-x_1)^2 - (y-y_1)^2)}.$$

If the sphere lies in the positive z-axis then the visible hemisphere is defined by:

$$Z(x,y) = z_1 - \sqrt{(R^2 - (x-x_1)^2 - (y-y_1)^2)}.$$

We can replace the square root by a division by R. We then approximate the visible hemisphere by a paraboloid as discussed in [Fuch85]:

$$Z(x,y) = z_1 - (R^2 - (x-x_1)^2 - (y-y_1)^2)/R.$$

Z is of second degree in x and its evaluation will require two (horizontal) increments. The initial value of the first horizontal increment at position (x,y) is given by taking the *first differences* of Z for an N-step change in x:

$$
\begin{aligned}
\Delta Z_{0,\text{м}} &= Z_{1,\text{м}} - Z_{0,\text{м}} \\
&= Z(x+N,y) - Z(x,y) \\
&= (z_1 - (R^2 - ((x+N)-x_1)^2 - (y-y_1)^2)/R) - \\
&\quad (z_1 - (R^2 - (x-x_1)^2 - (y-y_1)^2)/R) \\
&= (2N/R)x + (N-2x_1)N/R.
\end{aligned}
$$

where $Z_{k,\text{м}} = Z(x+kN, y)$. The values of the constants $2N/R$ and $(N-2x_1)N/R$ are calculated in the controller and constant planar integers with their values are created. A planar integer with the initial values of the linear term, $(2N/R)x$, is calculated in one of the ways described in §3.2.2.

The value of the (constant) second horizontal increment can be derived by taking (any) *second differences* of Z:

$$
\begin{aligned}
\Delta^2 Z_{k,\text{м}} &= \Delta Z_{k+1,\text{м}} - \Delta Z_{k,\text{м}} \\
&= (Z_{k+2,\text{м}} - Z_{k+1,\text{м}}) - (Z_{k+1,\text{м}} - Z_{k,\text{м}}) \\
&= (Z(x+(k+2)N,y) - Z(x+(k+1)N,y)) - (Z(x+(k+1)N,y) - Z(x+kN,y)) \\
&= 2N^2/R.
\end{aligned}
$$

In a similar manner we can determine the values of the 2 vertical increments for the sphere.

3.8. Comparison With Other Rendering Systems

There have been a number of proposals for special purpose parallel rendering architectures, see §1.5. For our comparison we have selected three architectures which are suitable for polygon rendering in particular. We have also included in the comparison the likely performance of a uniprocessor.

The comparison is based on the number of memory cycles because that is the performance bottleneck of rendering (the same basis was used for a comparison by Demetrescu [Deme85]). The architectures are compared in the rendering of 3 convex polygons with areas of $p=100$, $p=1000$ and $p=10000$ pixels respectively. We assume that the polygons are 4-sided and that their shape is roughly square so that their height and width are equal to $\sqrt{p}$ pixels.

It must be stressed from the outset that this comparison is hard and unfair and the resulting figures should therefore be taken with caution. It is hard because the systems compared are very different and performance estimates are not always available but must be deduced from the description of the systems. It is unfair because account is not taken of any functionality apart from the operations being compared. It is also unfair because the performance "units" used (number of memory cycles) fail to express other costs which are significant in some systems. Nevertheless we believe that some useful, if crude, facts can be extracted from the comparison.

Three rendering operations are compared. The first, filling, is the determination of the pixels inside a polygon and the update of the frame buffer locations representing the colour of these pixels. We assume that the depth of the frame buffer is $fd = 10$ bits. The second operation, hidden surface elimination (HSE), is the identification of the pixels at which a polygon is visible using the z-buffer HSE algorithm. Once the depth of a polygon at a pixel has been determined, one comparison and one assignment per pixel are required (to compare the depth of a polygon at a pixel against the z-buffer value for the pixel and update the z-buffer value if necessary). The third operation, smooth shading (SS), determines a shading value for each pixel inside a polygon by linear interpolation (Gouraud shading). If colour shading is used, which is what we assume here, then 3 separate linear interpolations must be carried out, one for each of the 3 colour components.

The estimated number of memory cycles required by each architecture for each of the 3 polygon areas are given in the table below. The left figure of each triplet represents the filling cost, the middle one is the cost for HSE and the one on the right is the SS cost.

Rendering architecture	Number of pixels per polygon		
	100	1000	10000
M-bit Uniprocessor	100 750 750	1K 7.5K 7.5K	10K 75K 75K
Pixel-Planes	80 40 60	80 40 60	80 40 60
SLAM	2 NA 60 ?	3 NA 60 ?	7 NA 60 ?
Clark & Hannah	5 NA NA ?	25 NA NA ?	182 NA NA ?
32x32xM Processor Array	132 41 95	159 59 112	323 164 210

Fill HSE SS cycles   (NA: Not Applicable)

The question marks after the figures for the SLAM and the Clark & Hannah displays refer to the fact that these systems are likely to incur significant synchronisation and computation costs which are not accounted for in the memory cycle figures.

We begin by considering the performance of a uniprocessor whose word length, M, is at least as long as the maximum arithmetic precision used. Filling will cost about 1 memory cycle per pixel. HSE will require 1 addition, 1 comparison and 1 assignment (to the z-buffer) per pixel while SS will cost 3 additions per pixel (one for each of the 3 colour components being interpolated). An addition costs 2.5 cycles (one Read and one Read/Modify/Write cycle which is assumed to be 1.5 times longer than a normal memory cycle), a comparison costs 3 cycles and an assignment costs 2 cycles.

Pixel-planes implements all 3 rendering operations by evaluating linear functions. Each linear function is evaluated at all the pixels of image space simultaneously using two linear function evaluation trees. We have assumed that it takes about 20 cycles to evaluate a linear function over the whole image space using Pixel-planes [Fuch85].

The SLAM approach [Deme85] claims to be capable of filling a polygon in $\lceil \sqrt{p}/16 \rceil$ cycles by accessing the pixels of 16 scan-lines in one cycle. In an fd bit/pixel SLAM system, the number of rows of SLAMs is multiplied by fd and a linear function evaluation tree is added to each SLAM for intensity interpolation (smooth shading). Since $fd=10$ and assuming that the depth of each linear function evaluation tree is also about 10, the number of cycles needed to evaluate a linear function over the $\sqrt{p}$ scan-line height of a polygon will be $\lceil \sqrt{p}/(16*fd) \rceil * (fd+10)$. In other words $3* \lceil \sqrt{p}/(16*fd) \rceil *20$ cycles will be required for smooth (colour) shading.

Clark and Hannah's system [Clar80] consists of 64 processors (R-IMP's) organised in 8 columns. Each column is controlled by a column processor (C-IMP) and the C-IMP's are controlled by a "parent" processor. The frame buffer memory is interlaced among the R-IMP's. To fill a polygon, the parent processor sorts the vertices of the polygon according to their x-coordinates and passes pairs of edges to the C-IMP's which, in turn, determine vertical spans of pixels to be filled and pass this information to the R-IMP's of their columns which modify the frame buffer. The number of frame buffer memory accesses required in order to fill a polygon is thus equal to the number of windows intersected by the polygon which is $(\sqrt{p}/N+1)^2$ but this does not take into account the cost of the computations and the communications between the various processors.

The performance of the rendering algorithms presented in this Chapter will be based on a 32×32×M processor array, where $M \geq pd, fd, zd$ so that planar arithmetic as well as assignments to the frame and depth buffers can be performed bit-parallel. The number of memory cycles for filling, HSE and SS are found by substituting the appropriate values in the expressions we derived for T_{FILL}, T_{HSE} and T_{SS} in previous sections. The substitutions necessary are $(\sqrt{p}/N+1)^2$ for w, 32 for N, 4 for n and 1 for $\lceil pd/M \rceil$, $\lceil fd/M \rceil$ and $\lceil zd/M \rceil$.

Although the comparison is crude, some useful facts can be derived from it. First, the performance of our rendering algorithms on a general purpose processor array is far better than the performance of a uniprocessor but lags behind the performance of special purpose architectures. Second, some of the special purpose architectures do not provide the functionality that is necessary in order to perform all of the three rendering operations that we considered.

3.9. Conclusion

In this Chapter we have shown how a processor array can efficiently evaluate bivariate linear functions and thus implement rendering operations. Cheap, incremental, computation is thus exploited in conjunction with parallelism on a parallel architecture which has come to be recognised as general purpose. Our algorithms map very naturally onto the processor array because they are based on the window which is the processor array's primitive graphical object. The evaluation method can be extended to non-linear functions at a cost which is dependent on the order of the function.

Chapter 4
Parallel Polygon Rendering With Precomputed Surface Patches

4.1. Introduction

In Chapter 3 we have demonstrated how a processor array can perform polygon rendering operations by using planar arithmetic in order to evaluate linear functions. The implementation of the hidden surface elimination and smooth shading operations require respectively the evaluation of one and three linear functions over the relevant windows (assuming colour shading). The filling operation requires the evaluation of n linear functions (where n is the number of sides of the polygon being rendered). Thus at least 3/7 of the linear function evaluations were used for the filling operation since $n \geq 3$. Furthermore, only the sign planes of the evaluations of the n linear functions were required.

Linear function evaluations are costly when a bit-serial processor array is used (see figures of §3.2.6) and in the case of the filling operation they can be avoided since we are only interested in the sign planes. The sign plane of the evaluation of a linear function within a window consists of either:

  i. all 0's or all 1's corresponding to the cases when the line does not intersect the window, or
  ii. both 0's and 1's in a pattern that represents the intersection of a window with a halfplane (see figure 4.2). This pattern will from now on be referred to as a *surface patch* or *patch*.

The surface patches for a finite set of slopes of the linear function can be *precomputed* and stored as planar Booleans in the memory of the processor array. In this Chapter we present an algorithm which can "stitch-together" the appropriate surface patches in order to construct an instance of a restricted form of convex polygon (a trapezium). The evaluation of the n linear functions for filling can thus be avoided at the cost of some sequential code overheads (the "stitching" algorithm).

Since an arbitrary polygon can be divided into trapezia by "cutting" it at the horizontal lines that pass through its vertices / edge crossings (figure 4.1), our algorithm can be used to fill arbitrary polygons. *Trapezium* will refer a closed quadrilateral with two sides parallel to the x-axis of image space. Any of the sides may be of zero length.

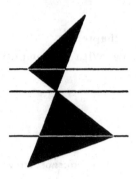

Figure 4.1. Dividing a polygon into trapezia

A variety of algorithms exist for the partitioning of simple polygons into trapezia (the case of convex polygons is particularly simple and obvious). Asano and Asano [Asan83] for instance, have developed an $O(n \log n)$ and an $O(n^3)$ algorithm for the partitioning of polygons into trapezia and minimum number of trapezia respectively. If the partitioning of polygons into trapezia turns out to be a bottleneck of the rendering process, parallel algorithms can be designed to perform the partitioning on the transputer network of the Disputer.

In this Chapter we deal only with the problem of filling trapezia which have pixel-aligned vertices for simplicity of explanation. The method can readily be extended to subpixel vertices at the cost of additional precomputed patches.

4.2. Two Approaches and Our Choice

We use precomputed surface patches to construct the part of the trapezium enclosed in the relevant windows (RW's) that are intersected by the sides of the trapezium. The interior of the trapezium is filled by simple application of the RasterOp primitive.

Before starting the filling process we create the surface patches. Each surface patch is a planar Boolean that represents the intersection of the "inside" halfplane defined by one side of the trapezium with an RW (figure 4.2). We compute one surface patch for each of a finite set of slopes in octants 1 through 4. The number of patches required for a particular accuracy is derived in §4.5. We only need to compute patches for octants 1 to 4.

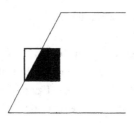

Figure 4.2. Example patch for left side in octant 2

All patches for a particular octant originate from the same corner of the window. The shifting (planar word shift) and masking (conditional planar assignment) operations of the processor array are used to transform the patches appropriately.

4.2.1. The Patch-First Approach

This approach completely ignores the RW's. It constructs the trapezium by positioning the appropriate sequences of surface patches along each of the two sides and then filling the area between them (figure 4.3).

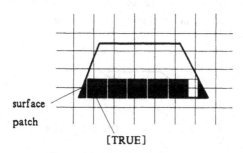

Figure 4.3. The patch-first approach

This approach has a number of drawbacks:

α. For efficiency, it requires *quadrant addressing* in the processor array [Spro83]; the ability to access a bit-aligned memory plane in one (rather than four) memory cycles. This facility is not generally available on current processor arrays.

β. It gives rise to several algorithmic complications:

β1. If one side of the trapezium lies in octants 1 or 4 and the other in octants 2 or 3, or if both sides are in octants 1 or 4, then the y-increment of the surface patches will be different for the two sides (figure 4.4). This makes filling the area between the two sides much harder as the two sides must be treated separately.

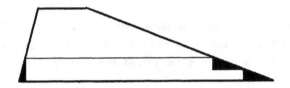

Figure 4.4. The problem of sides in different octants

β2. The area between the patches of the two sides will not, as a rule, be a multiple of N as figure 4.3 shows. We can not therefore use an integer number of window-sized RasterOp's to fill this area.

β3. Dealing with trapezia whose sides overlap in their x-extents is not straightforward. The patches that we use for one side may extend beyond the other side (figure 4.5). Some way of intersecting the patches for the two sides is required.

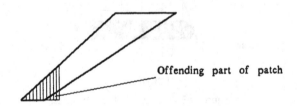

Offending part of patch

Figure 4.5. The problem of horizontally overlapping sides

4.2.2. The RW-First Approach

The RW-first approach visits the RW's (figure 4.6) in some order which is dependent on the octants that the trapezium's sides lie in and, using the precomputed patches, creates the *COVER.MASK* that corresponds to the part of the trapezium that intersects each RW.

69

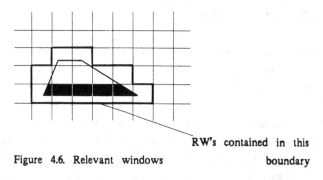

RW's contained in this
Figure 4.6. Relevant windows   boundary

By considering each RW separately we avoid all the problems of the patch-first approach but two new problems arise:

α. There is no single order of visiting the RW's that can handle both sides in all four octants. In fact, we need four different processing orders (§4.3.1).

β. We can not use Sproull's simple N-step line generating algorithm [Spro82] to trace out the sides of our trapezium. (An N-step line generating algorithm generates one point of the line for every N-step change in the variable that represents the direction of greatest motion; it is a generalisation of Bresenham's line generating algorithm [Bres65]). We can not use it because we have to start at the appropriate window boundary (intersected by the extrapolation of the trapezium's side) rather than the beginning of the side itself, see figure 4.7. Such an algorithm is developed in §4.4 using program transformations.

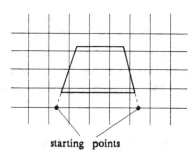

starting points
Figure 4.7. Starting points for our multipoint Bresenham

We have chosen to develop the RW-first algorithm both for its wider applicability (it does not assume quadrant addressing) and for its (relative) algorithmic simplicity.

4.3. The RW-First Algorithm

We shall assume for the moment that both sides of the trapezium lie in the first octant. The cases when both sides lie in any other octant are similar. The extension required to cater for the sides being in different octants is discussed in §4.3.1.

The RW's are processed one row at a time. The RW's of a row of windows are identified by the coordinates produced by the two N-step Bresenhams which are used to trace the left and right sides of the trapezium (see §4.4). Thus it is not necessary to inspect the *COVER.MASK* in order to identify the RW's (this was the method proposed for identifying the RW's in the filling method which is based on linear function evaluations, see §3.2.4). The rows of RW's are processed in Bottom → Top order and, when both sides of the trapezium lie in octant 1, the RW's within a row are processed in Left → Right order. The following actions are taken for each RW:

1. Check if the left side of the trapezium intersects the .RW. If it does:

    1.1. If the left edge of the RW is intersected by the left side of the trapezium:

        1.1.1. Derive the intersection of the left side of the trapezium with the right edge of the RW (or the extension of the right edge) using the N-step Bresenham (§4.4). Thus, by considering the difference between the y-coordinates of the intersections of the left side of the trapezium with the left and right edges of the RW respectively, choose between the two surface patches that approximate the slope of the left side of the trapezium.

        1.1.2. Transform the selected surface patch by shifting it up to the point where the left side intersects the left edge of the current RW, inserting TRUE's from below (first transformation of figure 4.8). Save the part of the patch that "overflows" out of the top of the current RW (if any) in a planar Boolean called "ready patch" for the RW above.

    1.2. If the bottom edge of the RW is intersected by the left side of the trapezium then a "ready patch" exists for this RW. A patch-fetch and a patch-shift operation (steps 1.1.1. and 1.1.2.) are thus saved.

2. Repeat similarly for the right side of the trapezium.

3. If both sides of the trapezium intersect the RW then logically AND their patches to create the *COVER.MASK* for the RW else

> If only one side intersects the RW then the *COVER.MASK* for the RW is the patch of the intersecting side else

>> The RW is surrounded by the trapezium (possibly intersected by the bases), and the *COVER.MASK* for the RW is assigned the constant planar Boolean [TRUE].

4. If one or both of the bases of the trapezium intersect(s) the RW then clear (set to FALSE) the horizontal top (bottom) strip of the *COVER.MASK* that extends above (below) the y-coordinate of the intersecting base(s) - the second transformation shown in figure 4.8.

5. Write the *COVER.MASK* into the frame buffer bitplane corresponding to the current RW. Colour may be introduced by using the *COVER.MASK* for the RW and the appropriate logical function in order to update each of the fd bitplanes of the frame buffer that correspond to the current RW.

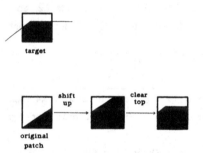

Figure 4.8. Patch transformations

4.3.1. Order of Visiting the RW's

The order of visiting the RW's matters because we only know one intersector RW for each of the two sides of the trapezium at any time. This is because the N-step Bresenham is not advanced past this RW until we visit it. If we therefore visit an RW which intersects a side of the trapezium before we have advanced the N-step Bresenham of the side to that RW, we shall miss the fact that the RW is intersected by that side. An alternative method is to generate a list of all intersecting RW's for both sides of the trapezium before visiting the RW's which requires extra space to store the intersections.

The order of visiting the RW's depends on the octant that a side lies in. For octants 1 and 2 the order is Bottom → Up, Left → Right and for octants 3 and 4 it is Bottom → Up, Right → Left. If one of the sides lies in octants 1 or 2 and the other in octants 3 or 4 then we have to split the trapezium about a vertical line, which for convenience can pass through one of the vertices of the trapezium, and process the RW's of each part in a different order (figure 4.9).

(a) Both sides in octants 1,2. Order is Left–Right, Bottom–Up

(b) Both sides in octants 3,4. Order is Right–Left, Bottom–Up

(c) Left side in octants 3,4 right side in octants 1,2. Split trapezium and use Right–Left order for left part, Left–Right order for right part (Bottom–Up)

(d) Left side in octants 1,2 right side in octants 3,4. Split trapezium and use Left–Right order for left part, Right–Left order for right part (Bottom–Up)

Figure 4.9. Order of visiting the RW's

4.4. The N-step Line Generating Algorithm

Once again, we shall restrict our discussion to octant 1 for simplicity of explanation. Given the endpoints (x_1,y_1) and (x_2,y_2) in screen coordinates of a line segment (a side of the trapezium), we need to modify Sproull's N-step line generating algorithm [Spro82] so that it starts from the point of intersection (x_3,y_3) of the left extrapolation of the line segment and the first vertical window boundary that it meets (figure 4.10).

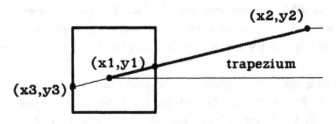

Figure 4.10. N-step Bresenham starting at a window boundary

More precisely, (x_3, y_3) must satisfy:

$$x_3 = \lfloor x_1 / N \rfloor * N$$
$$y_3 = y_1 - (x_1 - x_3) * ((y_2 - y_1) / (x_2 - x_1))$$

and the starting point (pixel) of our N-step algorithm should be $(x_3, \lfloor y_3 + 1/2 \rfloor)$.

We have used mathematical and program transformations to derive an efficient algorithm (no multiplications, divisions or reals) which implements our requirements from a very simple but obviously correct version using a method similar to Sproull's [Spro82]. The correctness of each transformation step guarantees the correctness of the final, efficient version. This derivation is reported here since it produced in a few hours a correct algorithm which eluded the author's informal efforts for some considerable time.

Here is the simple version of the N-step line generating algorithm which obviously implements our requirements in an imaginary version of Occam that includes infinite precision reals (type XREAL). No rounding or truncating need be specified when converting other types into XREAL:

Version 1

```
XREAL y3:
...INT all other variables
SEQ
    x3 := (x1 / N) * N            --/ rounds down since x1, N ≥ 0
    c := x1 - x3
    y3 := (XREAL y1) - ((XREAL c) * ((XREAL dy) / (XREAL dx)))

    SEQ i = 0 FOR ((x2-x3)/N)+1   --/ rounds down since (x2-x3), N ≥ 0
        SEQ
            xi := x3 + (i * N)
            yi := INT TRUNC (y3 + (((XREAL (xi - x3))
                    * ((XREAL dy) / (XREAL dx))) + (0.5 (XREAL))))
            display (xi, yi)
```

The multiplications in the calculations of xi and yi can be avoided by computing them incrementally. Hence we get the next version:

Version 2

XREAL $y3$:

...INT all other variables

SEQ

    $x3 := (x1 \ / \ N) \ * \ N$

    $c := x1 - x3$

    $y3 := (\text{XREAL } y1) - ((\text{XREAL } c) \ * \ ((\text{XREAL } dy) \ / \ (\text{XREAL } dx)))$

    SEQ $i = 0$ FOR $((x2 - x3) \ / \ N) + 1$

      SEQ

        $xi := x3$

        $yi := \text{INT TRUNC } (y3 + (0.5 \ (\text{XREAL})))$

        display $(xi, \ yi)$

        $x3 := x3 + N$

        $y3 := y3 + [((\text{XREAL } N) \ * \ ((\text{XREAL } dy) \ / \ (\text{XREAL } dx)))]$

(Square brackets delimit expressions whose values should be computed once only, outside the loop). We can save one addition per loop in the calculation of yi by substituting $y4 = y3 + 0.5$:

Version 3

XREAL $y4$:

...INT all other variables

SEQ

    $x3 := (x1 \ / \ N) \ * \ N$

    $c := x1 - x3$

    $y4 := ((\text{XREAL } y1) - ((\text{XREAL } c) \ * \ ((\text{XREAL } dy) \ / \ (\text{XREAL } dx))))$

                                       $+ \ (0.5 \ (\text{XREAL}))$

    SEQ $i = 0$ FOR $((x2 - x3) \ / \ N) + 1$

      SEQ

        $xi := x3$

        $yi := \text{INT TRUNC } (y4)$

        display $(xi, \ yi)$

        $x3 := x3 + N$

        $y4 := y4 + [((\text{XREAL } N) \ * \ ((\text{XREAL } dy) \ / \ (\text{XREAL } dx)))]$

We next split $y4$ into $y4i$, its integral part, and $y4f$, its fractional part, such that:

$$y4 = y4i + y4f.$$

$N * (dy / dx)$, the $y4$ increment, may also have integer and fractional parts; let t stand for its integral part so that:

$$0 \leq N * (dy / dx) - t < 1.$$

A suitable value for t is $\lfloor N * (dy / dx) \rfloor$ and should be precomputed:

Version 4

```
XREAL y4f:
...INT all other variables
SEQ
    t := N * (dy / dx)    --/ rounds down as dx, dy ≥ 0 (octant 1)
    x3 := (x1 / N) * N
    c := x1 - x3
    y4f := ((XREAL y1) - ((XREAL c) * ((XREAL dy) / (XREAL dx))))
                                              + (0.5 (XREAL))
    y4i := INT TRUNC (y4f)
    y4f := y4f - (XREAL y4i)

    SEQ i = 0 FOR ((x2 - x3) / N) + 1
        SEQ
            xi := x3
            display (xi, y4i)
            x3 := x3 + N
            IF
                (y4f + [(((XREAL N) * ((XREAL dy) / (XREAL dx)))
                                    - (XREAL t))] ≥ (XREAL 1))
                    SEQ
                        y4i := y4i + [(t + 1)]
                        y4f := y4f + [(((XREAL N) * ((XREAL dy)
                              / (XREAL dx))) - (XREAL (t + 1)))]
                TRUE
                    SEQ
                        y4i := y4i + t
                        y4f := y4f + [(((XREAL N) * ((XREAL dy)
                              / (XREAL dx))) - (XREAL t))]
```

The calculation of the initial values of $y4i$ and $y4f$ can be done in a loop as follows:

```
SEQ
    y4i := yl
    y4f := (0.5 (XREAL))
    SEQ i = 0 FOR c
        IF
            (y4f - [((XREAL dy) / (XREAL dx))] < (XREAL 0))
                SEQ
                    y4i := y4i - 1
                    y4f := y4f - [(((XREAL dy) / (XREAL dx))
                                                    - (XREAL 1))]
            TRUE
                y4f := y4f - [((XREAL dy) / (XREAL dx))]
```

The fractional part $y4f$ can be eliminated by the substitution:

$$r = 2 * N * dy + 2 * (y4f - t - 1) * dx$$

(r is related to the error). The value:

$$a = 2 * N * dy - 2 * t * dx$$

is very useful, and we precompute it in the same loop as $t = \lfloor N * (dy/dx) \rfloor$, the minimal y-increment in N horizontal steps. We thus arrive at version 5:

Version 5

...INT all variables

--calculation of t and a (derived using similar Program Transformations)

SEQ
    $t := 0$
    $a := 0$
    $rtemp := dy - dx$
    SEQ $i := 0$ FOR N
       SEQ
          $a := a + [(2 * dy)]$
          IF
             $(rtemp \geq 0)$
               SEQ
                 $t := t + 1$
                 $a := a - [(2 * dx)]$
                 $rtemp := rtemp - [(dx - dy)]$
             TRUE
               $rtemp := rtemp + dy$

--calculation of r and $y4i$

SEQ
    $x3 := (x1 / N) * N$
    $c := x1 - x3$
    $y4i := y1$
    $r := a - dx$
    SEQ $i := 0$ FOR c
       IF
          $(r < [a + ((2 * dy) - (2 * dx))])$
             SEQ
               $y4i := y4i - 1$
               $r := r - [((2 * dy) - (2 * dx))]$
          TRUE
            $r := r - [(2 * dy)]$

```
--The main loop
SEQ i := 0 FOR ((x2 - x3) / N) + 1
    SEQ
        xi := x3
        display (xi, y4i)
        x3 := x3 + N
        IF
            (r ≥ 0)
                SEQ
                    y4i := y4i + [(t + 1)]
                    r := r - [((2 * dx) - a)]
            TRUE
                SEQ
                    y4i := y4i + t
                    r := r + a
```

The initialisation of the algorithm (calculation of t, a, r and $y4i$) requires a maximum of $2N-1$ steps (since the maximum value of c is $N-1$). We can easily modify the above to select between two surface patches of height t and $t+1$ respectively instead of displaying a point in every execution of the main loop. Furthermore the main loop can be replaced by a procedure which selects between the two surface patches and returns the new value of $y4i$ when called.

Note that Version 5 uses only integer variables and that all multiplications and divisions can be implemented using shifting and logical operators (assuming N to be a power of 2).

4.5. How Many Surface Patches?

Gupta showed [Gupt8la] that it is not possible for lines generated using 2 of the precomputed strokes with an N-step algorithm to be optimal; i.e. it is not possible to guarantee that such lines consist of the same sequence of pixels as lines generated by a single step algorithm. The discontinuities in the edges of lines generated by the N-step algorithm are somewhat disturbing visually but may be reduced to insignificance by computing strokes to subpixel accuracy (figure 4.11). The same holds true for precomputed patches.

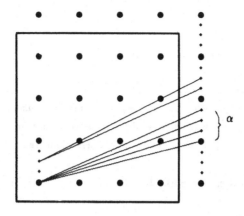

Figure 4.11. Subpixel accuracy (for $N = 4$)

Let α stand for the number of subpixel increments that we wish to use. (figure 4.11). There are $\alpha(\alpha N+1) = \alpha^2 N+\alpha$ different slopes for which we compute patches in each of the four octants, we therefore need to compute $4(\alpha^2 N+\alpha)$ patches. For $\alpha=4$, $N=16$ that implies 1040 patches or 1040 16x16 bitplanes of the memory of the processor array.

Notice that if we were to compute a patch for every possible RW-trapezium side intersection then many more patches would be needed. Instead we only compute patches emanating from the corner of a window and shift them to the intersection point. Furthermore, we saved a factor of 2 by only computing patches for one of the trapezium's sides. To get the patch for the other side with the same slope we use bitplane inversion (figure 4.12). Both bitplane shifting (planar word shift) and inversion (planar Boolean negation) are cheap operations on a processor array.

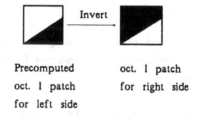

Precomputed   oct. 1 patch
oct. 1 patch   for right side
for left side

Figure 4.12. Bitplane inversion

The formula for the number of patches, $4(\alpha^2 N+\alpha)$, represents a trade-off between accuracy and time on one hand and space ($4(\alpha^2 N+\alpha)$) on the other. The larger our processor array (N), the fewer steps it will take to fill the trapezium but the larger the number (and the size) of the surface patches we need precompute. Similarly, the higher the accuracy we want (α) the greater the number of surface patches we must create.

4.6. Performance

The cost (time) of our algorithm is the sum of:

- The initialisation cost t_{INIT}.
- The cost of visiting an RW $(t_{IN} + t_{F.UPDATE})$ times the number of RW's (w).
- The extra cost for visiting an RW that intersects a side of the trapezium (t_{SIDE}) times the number of RW - trapezium side intersections (s).

The initialisation cost, t_{INIT}, consists of:

- Finding the slope of each side.
- Initialising the N-step Bresenhams for each side.
- Selecting the two surface patches best approximating each side and inverting them if necessary.
- Initialising the "ready patches", if necessary.

The minimum cost of processing an RW i.e. the cost of processing an RW that does not intersect a side of the trapezium is $t_{IN} + t_{F.UPDATE}$, where t_{IN} is the cost of:

- Initialising the $COVER.MASK$ of an RW.
- Clearing the top / bottom of the $COVER.MASK$ if needed (see figure 4.8).

$t_{F.UPDATE}$ is the cost of updating the part of the frame buffer that corresponds to the RW with the colour of the trapezium, see §3.2.6.

t_{SIDE} is the amount of time taken to:

- Advance the intersection points of the side using the N-step Bresenham.
- Choose one of the two surface patches approximating the side's slope and shift it as shown in figure 4.8.

It takes $t_{IN} + t_{F.UPDATE} + t_{SIDE}$ time to process an RW that is intersected by one of the trapezium's sides and $t_{IN} + t_{F.UPDATE} + 2t_{SIDE}$ to process an RW that is intersected by both sides of the trapezium. s is the number of RW - trapezium side intersections, see figure 4.13.

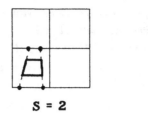
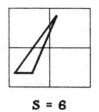

$$S = 2 \qquad\qquad S = 6$$

Figure 4.13. Value of s

The cost of filling a trapezium is then $t_{\text{INIT}} + w(t_{\text{IN}} + t_{\text{F.UPDATE}}) + s\, t_{\text{SIDE}}$. Thus the cost of filling an n-sided convex polygon, having broken it down into $n-1$ trapezia (the worst case), is:

$$T_{\text{FILL}} = (n-1)\, t_{\text{INIT}} + w(t_{\text{IN}} + t_{\text{F.UPDATE}}) + s\, t_{\text{SIDE}} \qquad\qquad (4.1)$$

where w and s refer to the number of RW's and number of RW – side intersections of the convex polygon respectively. We have ignored the fact that some RW's will be intersected by more than one of the trapezia that constitute the convex polygon and will therefore be visited more than once (increasing the values of w and s).

t_{INIT}, t_{IN} and t_{SIDE} can be broken down into sequential and processor array cost components. The estimation of the processor array cost can be done easily by counting the number of processor array memory cycles[1]. We have used an estimate of the number of store accesses as an indication of the sequential processor cost. The sequential and processor array cost components of t_{INIT}, t_{IN} and t_{SIDE} derived from our implementation follow:

	Array Cycles	Sequential Processor Store Accesses (Estimate)
t_{INIT}	8	1200 (1000 in N-step Bresenham initialisation)
t_{IN}	4	70
t_{SIDE}	3	40

---

1. The number of processor array cycles quoted, was obtained by efficient hand coding and optimising the processor array instructions. There was a significant difference between these figures and those resulting from the compilation of a high-level array language. In the latter case we had $t_{\text{INIT}} = 16$, $t_{\text{IN}} + t_{\text{F.UPDATE}} = 33$ and $t_{\text{SIDE}} = 8$ array cycles, but the high-level language proved invaluable in achieving the initial, correct code.

The cost of $t_{F.UPDATE}$ was given in Chapter 3. The large value of the sequential component of t_{INIT} is due to the initialisation of each of the two N-step Bresenhams which require between N and $2N-1$ steps, see §4.4. Thus the performance of rendering polygons that only span a few windows will be dominated by the large initialisation cost. The cost of filling a polygon depends (apart from its size) on its:

- Shape
- Position in the image space

as they both affect the values of w and s in (4.1). A long, thin polygon will take longer to fill than a fat one of the same area.

We shall now compare T'_{FILL} against T_{FILL}, the cost of filling a convex polygon using linear function evaluations as described in Chapter 3. In the following comparison we shall ignore the high sequential code overheads involved in T'_{FILL} and the comparison will be in terms of processor array cycles only.

We have seen in §3.2.6 that the number of processor array cycles in T_{FILL} is:

$$T_{FILL} = n((5\log_2 N + 5)\lceil pd/M \rceil) + 2.5n(w-1)\lceil pd/M \rceil + 2.5w\lceil fd/M \rceil.$$

If we make the assumption that $s = 2w$, then T'_{FILL} becomes:

$$T'_{FILL} = 8n + 10w - 8 + 2.5w\lceil fd/M \rceil \tag{4.2}.$$

To compare T'_{FILL} with T_{FILL} we shall consider two cases:

i. A bit-serial processor array and 16-bitplane deep planar arithmetic i.e. $\lceil pd/M \rceil = 16$.

ii. A bit-parallel processor array whose depth is equal to that of the planar arithmetic representation i.e. $\lceil pd/M \rceil = 1$.

In the first case, the expression for T_{FILL} becomes:

$$T_{FILL} = 80n\log_2 N + 40wn + 40n + 2.5w\lceil fd/M \rceil$$

and this is always greater than the expression for T'_{FILL} i.e. the precomputed patch filling method outperforms the linear evaluation filling method on a bit-serial processor array, as expected. This is true even when the planar arithmetic representation is only 16-bitplanes deep (an unrealistically low estimate, see §3.2.3).

In case ii. the expression for T_{FILL} becomes:

$$T_{\text{FILL}} = 5n\log_2 N \; + \; 2.5wn \; + \; 2.5n \; + \; 2.5w\lceil fd/M\rceil$$

and it is possible, for practical values of w, n and N, that $T_{\text{FILL}} < T'_{\text{FILL}}$ i.e. the precomputed patch filling method may be slower in this case. This is because the precomputed patch filling method can not utilise the depth of the bit-parallel processor array.

Finally we shall contrast T'_{FILL} against the performance of other proposed architectures given in the table of §3.8. The simplified expression for T'_{FILL} (equation 4.2) gives the following array cycle costs for filling polygons of 3 different sizes (the variables of T'_{FILL} are assigned the values that were assumed in §3.8):

	Number of pixels per polygon		
	100	1000	10000
T'_{FILL}	46 (132)	73 (159)	237 (323)

where the numbers in parentheses are the corresponding values of T_{FILL} given in the table of §3.8. Notice that a bit-parallel processor array was assumed in §3.8.

4.7. Texture Mapping

A texture map can be replicated within a trapezium at very little cost additional to filling the trapezium with a particular colour. The *COVER.MASK* for an RW is combined with a planar integer representing a texture map instead of a planar integer that represents a flat colour. This was explained in §3.4.1.

4.8. Anti-aliasing the Surface Patches

If a grey scale display is available, we can gain spatial resolution i.e. subpixel accuracy by trading off the colour (grey scale) resolution of the display; this is the colour / space resolution trade-off.

To make use of the j grey levels, the $\lceil\log_2 j\rceil$-bitplane deep surface patches are computed to an accuracy α s.t. $\alpha \geq j$ (see figure 4.11). As Gupta [Gupt81a] has shown in the case of precomputed strokes (line segments), the maximum grey scale error will asymptotically approach $1/(2j)$ as α is increased. For example, if $j = 4$ grey levels are available, then the maximum grey scale error e will range between $1/(2j)$ and $1/j$ depending on the value of α:

$$12.5\% \;<\; e \;<\; 25\% \qquad \text{for } j = 4.$$

The above discussion concerns the anti-aliasing of pixels that are partially covered by a single patch i.e. a single trapezium side. Anti-aliasing pixels that are partially covered by more than one patches (whether the patches belong to the same trapezium or not) is a significantly harder problem because it requires knowledge about the spatial coverage of the pixel by each of the patches. The anti-aliasing of the surface patches could be classified as a pre-filtering technique (see §1.3.4).

4.9. Is Precomputation of the Values of a Linear Function Feasible?

We have seen in Chapter 3 that the largest part of the cost of evaluating a linear function over a small number of image space windows using a processor array, comes from the initial evaluation over the first window. The evaluation over subsequent windows is carried out incrementally at a cost of 1 planar addition per window. We have also described a way of performing the initial evaluation with only $2\log_2 N$ planar additions; this is still about an order of magnitude more expensive than the cost of an incremental evaluation (for usual values of N i.e. 16, 32, 64).

The question then arises, would it be possible to speed-up the initial evaluation of a linear function by precomputation of the function's values, in a manner similar to the precomputation of the sign planes for filling? If this were possible, the cost of the initial evaluation of the linear functions used in HSE and SS could be reduced.

The value of the linear function $F(x,y) = ax + by + c$ at a pixel (x,y) within the initial window can be split into three additive components; the c value the ax value and the by value. It is the ax and by values that we would like to precompute for the coordinates of every pixel (x,y) within the initial window. The values of the linear function can range between 0 and $2^{pd}-1$ because the depth of the planar arithmetic representation is pd bitplanes deep. Therefore the maximum difference between the values of the linear function at two extreme pixels within the initial window which have the same x or y coordinate is $2^{pd}-1$. We must therefore precompute at least $2^{pd}-1$ pd-bitplane deep planar integers, one for each of the $2^{pd}-1$ possible values of aN, the first difference of the linear function for an N-step change in x. (It is possible to precompute the ax values to a higher accuracy, just like the surface patches could be precomputed to subpixel accuracy, at extra storage cost). By a similar argument, at least another $2^{pd}-1$ pd-bitplane deep planar integers will be needed for the precomputation of the by values of the linear function, making a total of $2(2^{pd}-1)$ pd-bitplane deep planar integers. The initial values of the linear function could then be computed by 2 planar additions of the appropriate ax and by precomputed planar integers to a planar integer containing the evaluation of the linear function for the bottom-left pixel of the initial window.

The number of bitplanes needed to store the precomputed planar integers is then at least $2(2^{pd}-1)pd$. Even for a planar arithmetic accuracy which is as low as $pd=16$, more than 2 million bitplanes are required and this is excessive. After all the saving is only $2\log_2 N$ $- 2 = 6$ planar additions per linear function evaluation if $N=16$.

4.10. Precomputed Spheres

Sections §3.7.1 and §3.7.2 describe how to fill and HSE spheres by evaluating bivariate quadratic functions. The view point invariant appeerence of a sphere makes it a good candidate for precomputation because only one view of it needs to be precomputed. Hubbard describes in [Hubb85] how to use the DAP in order to fill, HSE and SS spheres that are smaller than an $N\times N$ window.

For each one of a range of sphere radii, 3 planar entities are precomputed. A planar Boolean, *SPHERE*, contains TRUE only in those elements that are covered by a planar projection of the sphere. A planar integer, *SPHEREZ*, contains the height of each pixel element in the visible hemisphere above the XY plane, for a sphere with origin in the XY plane. Finally, planar integer *SPHEREI* contains the intensity of each pixel on the visible hemisphere for a particular light source position. At run-time, the distance of the desired sphere from the view point is used to select the precomputed sphere with the appropriate radius. The distance is then added to each element of *SPHEREZ* giving a planar integer that contains the true distance of each pixel on the visible hemisphere of the desired sphere from the view point. *SPHERE*, *SPHEREZ* and *SPHEREI* are then shifted in x and y (using planar word shifts) so that the precomputed sphere centre coincides with the desired sphere centre relative to the window coordinates (planar shifts are cheap operations on a processor array). The sphere is finally rendered using the z-buffer algorithm for HSE. The quadratic function evaluations can thus be saved.

4.11. Conclusion

An algorithm for the rapid filling of trapezia on a processor array has been presented in this Chapter. The algorithm can serve as the basis for filling arbitrary polygons, the case of convex polygons being particularly simple. It uses precomputed surface patches which represent the intersection of a window with a particular halfplane or equivalently the sign plane of the planar integer that contains the evaluation of a linear function within a window. Thus the linear function evaluations required in order to determine the *COVER.MASK* (i.e. the pixels of a window covered by a polygon) can be avoided and the performance of the filling operation on bit-serial processor arrays is significantly improved (on such machines planar arithmetic is costly). Bit-parallel processor arrays can not take full advantage of the method because the surface patches are single bitplanes. Precomputation gains extra speed by using additional storage space for the patches. This is an increasingly advantageous trade-off with decreasing memory prices. Program transformations proved an effective tool for constructing an efficient version of the particular N-step Bresenham we needed.

Chapter 5
Parallel Polygon Rendering on a Dual-Paradigm Parallel Processor

5.1. Introduction

The commonly used technique of divide and conquer can be effectively applied in the field of computer graphics. One way of rendering a complex scene, is to model it by a set of polygons and render each of its constituent polygons. The task of rendering the complex scene is split into the subtasks of dividing the complex scene into polygons and rendering each of the polygons; these two subtasks can be assigned to separate processors. Rendering represents a performance bottleneck in the graphics output pipeline, see for example [Theo85], and a simple rendering primitive is usually chosen (e.g. polygon) and implemented efficiently on the "rendering machine", i.e. the processor which is assigned the task of rendering.

In Chapter 4 the simple rendering primitive was chosen to be the trapezium. The rendering machine, an $N \times N$ SIMD array of bit-serial processors (processor array), used precomputed surface patches (intersections of windows with halfplanes, figure 5.1) to construct an arbitrary trapezium. The disparity between trapezia and surface patches gave rise to the large sequential code overhead of the algorithm. (The initialisation in particular was very costly). It is not simple to determine how to stitch up the surface patches in order to construct the required trapezium.

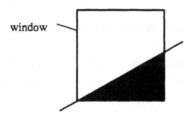

window

Figure 5.1. Surface patch (planar Boolean)

In this Chapter a further step is taken and an even simpler rendering primitive is chosen in order to reduce the sequential code overheads and thus increase the utilisation of the rendering machine (the processor array). In fact, the simplest rendering primitive that can be constructed out of precomputed surface patches is chosen: the surface patch itself! The task of the rendering machine is thus simplified to its limit and the task of dividing objects into surface patches is assigned to other processors.

5.2. Convex Polygon Filling on the Disputer

The intersection of a convex polygon with a window of image space is also a convex polygon (if not null) called a subwindow convex polygon, figure 5.2. For the rest of this Chapter, polygon will refer to a convex polygon and subwindow polygon will refer to a subwindow convex polygon.

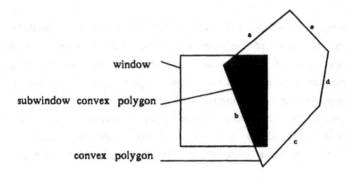

Figure 5.2. Subwindow convex polygon

A subwindow polygon can also be regarded as the intersection of a window with the halfplanes defined by the sides of the polygon intersecting the window (sides *a* and *b* in figure 5.2). A particular subwindow polygon can therefore be constructed by intersecting the appropriate precomputed surface patches (which represent the intersection of a window with a halfplane).

The task of rendering a polygon can be divided into two parts:

    1. *Splitting* i.e. the *determination* of the precomputed surface patches and transformations on them required for the construction of the subwindow polygons that make up the polygon, and

    2. *Rendering* i.e. the *execution* of the transformations on the appropriate patches as dictated in 1. above (*rendering* here is used as a synonym for *filling* but, as we shall see later in this Chapter, the method can be extended in order to handle other rendering operations such as HSE and SS).

It is only the latter task, rendering, that is assigned to the transputer which controls the processor array. The controller is thus relieved from the operations that do not involve the use of the processor array. The splitting task is assigned to another transputer. For the rest of this Chapter, the transputer which controls the processor array will be called the *renderer* while the transputer which is assigned the splitting task will be the *splitter*, figure 5.3.

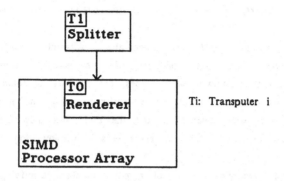

Ti: Transputer i

Figure 5.3. Splitter and renderer

More than one splitter transputers can be employed if splitting is the performance bottleneck of the two operations (this is the case in our implementation, see §5.3.2). Information is passed from the splitter to the renderer in accordance with a communication protocol described in §5.2.1. Sections 5.2.2 and 5.2.3 describe the task of the splitter and the renderer.

5.2.1. The Communication Protocol

The communication protocol between the splitter and the renderer will be described in a BNF-like notation. Terminals (i.e. variables or constant values that are actually communicated) are in lower case italics and the number of bytes required for them is denoted by a subscript. A dash (-) between terminals means that they are transmitted in the same byte. Curly brackets ({ }) denote repetition, the number of times is superscripted; * means 0 or more times.

A polygon description is made up of a set of subwindow polygon descriptions plus extent and colour information:

$$\text{POLYGON} ::= extent.xmin_1\ extent.ymin_1$$
$$extent.xlength_1\ extent.ylength_1\ colour_1$$
$$\{\ \text{SUB.POLYGON}\ \}^{extent.xlength\ *\ extent.ylength}$$

There is a subwindow polygon description for each window in the extent but the protocol can easily be altered so that only relevant windows are included. The extent parameters specify the smallest rectangle of windows that includes the polygon. The dimensions of the extent are therefore given in windows. A subwindow polygon is defined as the intersection (Boolean ANDing) of a set of precomputed patches:

$$SUB.POLYGON ::= \{ next.patch_1 \; PATCH \}^n \; prev.window.coverage_1$$

The special value *next.patch* separates adjacent patch descriptions while *prev.window.coverage* can take on one of two possible values which are used to distinguish between those subwindow polygons that partially or totally cover a window and those that do not intersect at all (both totally covering and non-intersecting subwindow polygons have zero patch descriptions and the two cases must therefore be distinguished). The *prev.window.coverage* value also serves as a subwindow polygon description separator.

The 2-byte patch description consists of a patch number, identifying the patch to be used, and 3 parameters that specify how the patch must be transformed (an invert bit and the shift amount and direction). As mentioned in Chapter 4, a large saving in the number of precomputed patches is made by employing two cheap, run-time patch transformations (invertion and shifting):

$$PATCH ::= patch.no-invert_1 \quad shift.dir-shift.amt_1 \; .$$

5.2.2. Subwindow Polygon Rendering on a Processor Array

A set of surface patches, representing the intersection of a window with a halfplane whose defining line can have any of a finite number of slopes in octants 1 through 4, is precomputed and stored in the memory of the processor array. The number of surface patches required for a particular accuracy is derived in §4.5.

The renderer receives from the splitter, the sequence of patch descriptions required in order to construct the subwindow polygons for each window in the extent of the polygon. A patch description consists of the following information:

- patch number (identification)
- shift direction (L,R,U,D – the direction to shift the patch)
- shift amount
- invert bit (indicates whether to invert the patch).

Patch descriptions belonging to the same subwindow polygon are grouped together so that the surface patches they describe can be ANDed together (a surface patch is a bitplane of the processor array (PLANAR.BOOL)). Figure 5.4 shows how patches A and B are transformed and then ANDed to construct a subwindow polygon.

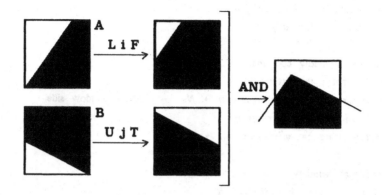

Figure 5.4. Constructing a subwindow convex polygon

Patch A is shifted L(eft) by i places while patch B is shifted U(p) by j places and then inverted (invert = T(rue)).

The subwindow polygon can be regarded as a mask, $COVER.MASK$, which identifies the pixels of a window covered by a polygon. In a black and white display, this mask is copied directly into the frame buffer bitplane which represents the relevant window. Colour or texture can be added very simply in the manner described in §3.4.1.

The renderer is next described in Occam. It is assumed that the polygon description has been input into one of a pair of global BYTE buffers which is identified by $buff.id$:

```
PROC render.from.buff (VAL INT buff.id)
   ... declarations
   PROC get.from.buff (INT x)
      SEQ
         x := INT (buff [buff.id] [buff.ptr])
         buff.ptr := buff.ptr + 1
   :
   SEQ
      buff.ptr := 0
```

```
--get extent and colour information from buffer
get.from.buff (extent.xmin)
get.from.buff (extent.ymin)
get.from.buff (extent.xlength)
get.from.buff (extent.ylength)
get.from.buff (colour)


--initialise window coordinates
window.xmin := extent.xmin
window.xmax := window.xmin + N        --N = window side
window.ymin := extent.ymin
window.ymax := window.ymin + N


--for each window in the extent
SEQ i = 0 FOR extent.ylength
   SEQ
      SEQ j = 0 FOR extent.xlength
         SEQ
            --initialise window COVER.MASK to TRUE
            COVER.MASK := PLANAR.BOOL (TRUE)

            get.from.buff (input)
            --for each patch of the subwindow polygon
            WHILE (input = next.patch)
               SEQ
                  ...get and transform precomputed patch
                  ...AND patch with COVER.MASK
                  get.from.buff (input)
            IF
               (input = prev.window.covered)
                  ...use COVER.MASK to render subwindow polygon
               TRUE
                  SKIP
            --update window coordinates
            window.xmin := window.xmax
            window.xmax := window.xmax + N
      window.xmin := extent.xmin
      window.xmax := window.xmin + N
      window.ymin := window.ymax
      window.ymax := window.ymax + N
```

Input of polygon descriptions is handled by another process, *input.to.buff*. Two measures are taken to make the communication efficient:

1. Array slice communication rather than element-by-element communication is used. For reasonably large array slices, the former type of communication is about 34% faster than the latter [Wind88] because the communication setup cost is only paid once for each array slice. A polygon description is packed into a single array slice.

2. Input and rendering are overlapped since transputer links can operate in parallel with the processor. This is achieved by inputting the next polygon description in parallel with the rendering of the current one. Two polygon description buffers are thus used.

The following Occam processes encapsulate the above:

```
PROC render (CHAN in)
    ...PROC render.from.buff (VAL INT buff.id)      --described above
    ...PROC input.to.buff (VAL INT buff.id, INT length)    --below

    VAL max.buff IS
    VAL buff.0    IS 0:
    VAL buff.1    IS 1:
    [2] [max.buff] BYTE buff:
    [2] INT buff.length:
    INT buff.ind:

    SEQ
        ...initialisations
        buff.ind := 0
        input.to.buff (buff.0, buff.length[buff.0])

        WHILE TRUE
            IF
                (buff.ind = buff.0)
                    SEQ
                        PAR
                            input.to.buff (buff.1, buff.length[buff.1])
                            render.from.buff (buff.0)
                        buff.ind := buff.1
```

```
        TRUE    --(buff.ind  =  buff.1)
           SEQ
              PAR
                 input.to.buff  (buff.0,  buff.length[buff.0])
                 render.from.buff  (buff.1)
              buff.ind  :=  buff.0
     :
```

Where *input.to.buff* is defined as:

```
     PROC input.to.buff (VAL INT buff.id, INT length)
        BYTE length.byte:
        SEQ
           in ? length.byte
           length := INT (length.byte)
           in ? [buff [buff.id] FROM 0 FOR length]
     :
```

5.2.3. Splitting Polygons Into Subwindow Polygons - Determination of the Surface Patches

As mentioned above, the splitting task is assigned to a transputer which operates in parallel with the processor array (figure 5.3).

A subwindow polygon is represented by a set of patch descriptions; one for each side of the polygon intersecting the window (it is not necessary to use surface patches for the sides of the subwindow convex polygon that coincide with the window boundaries). The splitter can therefore determine the patch descriptions required to make up the subwindow polygon that represents the intersection of its polygon with a particular window, by clipping each side of its polygon against the window. Thus it uses line clipping rather than polygon clipping which is a more complex process. The coordinates of the points of intersection of each side of the polygon with the window are rounded to the accuracy of the precomputed surface patches (e.g. to the nearest pixel coordinates if no subpixel accuracy is used) and are then used to determine the appropriate surface patch as well as the shift amount and direction. In order to determine whether the surface patch must be inverted, information is required as to which of the two halfplanes - that the side of the polygon divides the polygon's plane - the polygon lies in. If the vertices of the polygon are considered in an anticlockwise traversal around it, see figure 5.5, then the polygon lies to the left of its directed sides.

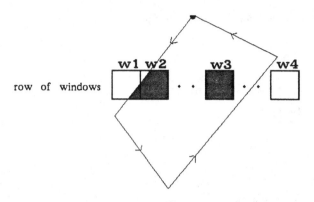

row of windows

Figure 5.5. It is useful to order the vertices of a polygon
according to an anticlockwise traversal around it

A further advantage of ordering the vertices of a polygon as shown in figure 5.5 is in
distinguishing between windows such as w3 and w4 in figure 5.5. Neither of these windows
is intersected by a side of the polygon and line clipping alone can not distinguish between
them, although one is totally covered by the polygon and the other is disjoint. However
the windows that make up the polygon's extent are considered in a particular order by
the splitter (e.g. bottom→top, left→right) and, by counting the number of times the
perimeter of the polygon has been intersected by a horizontal row of windows, it is
possible to decide whether a window that is not intersected by a side of the polygon is
totally covered (perimeter intersected once) or disjoint (perimeter intersected 0 or 2 times).
A difficulty arises when horizontally successive windows intersect the same part of the
polygon's perimeter. In figure 5.5 for example, w1 and w2 intersect the same (left) part
of the polygon's perimeter and the number of intersections of the polygon with this
particular row of windows should not be made equal to 2 when w2 is considered.
Fortunately, this difficulty can be overcome by using the anticlockwise ordering of the
polygon's vertices. The number of intersections of a row of windows with the polygon is
only made equal to 2 when an "upward" side is found to intersect the row of windows
(an upward side is one for which the y-coordinate of its finishing vertex is greater than
that of its starting vertex).

In the following Occam splitter process it is assumed that the coordinates of the vertices of
the polygon are globally available. They could either have been input from a channel or
derived by a viewing transformation from the original coordinates of the polygon's vertices.
The output of the process is stored in one of a pair of global BYTE buffers indicated
by buff.id:

```
PROC split.to.buff (VAL INT buff.id, INT buff.ptr)
  ...declarations
  PROC put.in.buff (VAL INT x)
    SEQ
      buff [buff.id] [buff.ptr] := BYTE (x)
      buff.ptr := buff.ptr + 1
  :


  SEQ
    buff.ptr := 0
    ...determine extent of polygon
    put.in.buff (extent.xmin)
    put.in.buff (extent.ymin)
    put.in.buff (extent.xlength)
    put.in.buff (extent.ylength)
    put.in.buff (colour)


    --initialise window coordinates
    window.xmin := extent.xmin
    window.xmax := window.xmin + N      --N = window side
    window.ymin := extent.ymin
    window.ymax := window.ymin + N


    --for each window in the extent
    SEQ i = 0 FOR extent.ylength
      SEQ
        SEQ j = 0 FOR extent.xlength
          SEQ
            --for each edge of the polygon
            SEQ k = 0 FOR n
              SEQ
                ...clip edge[k] against window
                ...use clipped line segment (if any) to determine
                            patch number & transformation parameters
                ...put patch number & transformation parameters
                                    (if any) in buff [buff.id]
```

```
              IF
                 window.partially.or.totally.covered.by.polygon
                    put.in.buff (prev.window.covered)
                 TRUE
                    put.in.buff (prev.window.uncovered)

                 --update window coordinates
                 window.xmin := window.xmax
                 window.xmax := window.xmax + N
           window.xmin := extent.xmin
           window.xmax := window.xmin + N
           window.ymin := window.ymax
           window.ymax := window.ymax + N
      :
```

As was the case in the renderer, buffering is used in order to overlap the computation of the splitter with output of polygon descriptions:

```
    PROC split (CHAN out)
      ... PROC split.to.buff (VAL INT buff.id, INT buff.ptr)   --above
      ... PROC output.from.buff (VAL INT buff.id, length)
          --output.from.buff is similar to input.to.buff

      ... body of split is similar to body of render
      :
```

Having defined the renderer and the splitter, we next make them components of the same PLACED PAR (the link configurations are not shown):

```
    CHAN c:
    PLACED PAR
       split (c)
       render (c)
```

5.3. Performance

The performance of the polygon rendering system described so far is limited by 3 independent factors:

1. The speed at which the renderer (the processor array) can transform and render the surface patches according to the polygon descriptions it receives from the splitter.

2. The rate at which the splitter can construct polygon descriptions.

3. The transputer link data rate available for the transmission of the polygon descriptions from the splitter to the renderer.

The overall performance of the system is determined by the tightest of the above three constraints (the bottleneck). The next three sections discuss each of the above factors.

5.3.1. Processor Array Rendering Performance

Assume that the simple change necessary to avoid the consideration of the non-relevant windows of a polygon's extent has been implemented in the communication protocol and the splitting and rendering algorithms of §5.2.2 and §5.2.3. Then the cost of filling a polygon which has w relevant windows and whose sides intersect s windows, see figure 5.6, on the processor array using the polygon description is:

$$T''_{FILL} = w * (t_{WINDOW} + t_{F.UPDATE}) + s * t_{PATCH}$$

where

t_{WINDOW} is the cost of initialising the *COVER.MASK* for a window and updating the coordinates of the current window.

$t_{F.UPDATE} = 2.5\lceil fd/M \rceil$ is the time required to update the part of the frame buffer corresponding to a window, see §3.2.6.

t_{PATCH} is the time taken to select and transform a patch according to a patch description and AND the result with the *COVER.MASK* of a window.

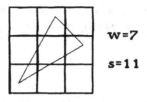

Figure 5.6. w and s

t_{WINDOW} and t_{PATCH} can be broken down into array cycles and an estimate of the number of sequential store accesses of the transputer renderer for comparison with the filling algorithms described in Chapters 3 and 4:

	Array Cycles	Sequential Processor Store Accesses (estimate)
t_{WINDOW}	1	20
t_{PATCH}	3.5	40

Let us now compare T''_{FILL} with T_{FILL} and T'_{FILL}, the performances of the filling algorithms of Chapters 3 and 4 respectively. It can be seen from the expression for T''_{FILL} above that the initialisation cost has been eliminated when compared to T'_{FILL}. The initialisation cost had a large sequential overhead which has now been assigned to the splitter. But even if T''_{FILL} and T'_{FILL} are compared in terms of processor array cycles only (thus ignoring the low sequential overheads of T''_{FILL}), T''_{FILL} will be smaller provided that:

$$(1 + 2.5\lceil fd/M\rceil)w + 3.5s < 8(n-1) + (4 + 2.5\lceil fd/M\rceil)w + 3s$$

or,

$$s < 16(n-1) + 6w$$

which will nearly always be true (it takes a very "awkward" convex polygon to make the above condition false).

When compared with T_{FILL}, the cost of filling a polygon using the incremental method of Chapter 3, T''_{FILL} will be smaller if:

$$(1 + 2.5\lceil fd/M\rceil)w + 3.5s < (n(5\log_2 N + 5) + 2.5n(w-1))\lceil pd/M\rceil + 2.5w\lceil fd/M\rceil$$

or,

$$8w < (n(5\log_2 N + 5) + 2.5n(w-1))\lceil pd/M\rceil$$

assuming that $s=2w$. If we give n, N and $\lceil pd/M \rceil$ their minimum values in order to minimise the rhs, i.e. $n=3$, $N=2$, $\lceil pd/M \rceil =1$, the above comparison becomes:

$$w < 45$$

in other words T''_{FILL} will be smaller than T_{FILL} if $w < 45$. However this is based on extreme values of n, N and $\lceil pd/M \rceil$. If $\lceil pd/M \rceil > 1$ or $n>3$, T''_{FILL} will be less than T_{FILL} for all values of w. The processor array can therefore achieve better performance in filling convex polygons with the help of the splitter provided that the other two factors (i.e. the performance of the splitter and the communication cost) do not present a bottleneck.

Let us now contrast T''_{FILL} against the performance of other proposed architectures given in the table of §3.8. Assuming that $s=2w$, T''_{FILL} gives the following array cycle costs for filling polygons of three different sizes (the variables of T''_{FILL} are assigned the values that were assumed in §3.8):

Number	of	pixels	per	polygon
	100	1000	10000	

T''_{FILL}	18(132)	42(159)	179(323)

where the numbers in parentheses are the corresponding values of T_{FILL} given in the table of §3.8. Notice that a bit-parallel processor array was assumed in §3.8.

5.3.2. Rendering Versus Splitting Performance

We have used a "supervisor" process to measure the utilisation of the splitter and renderer transputers. The concept of processor utilisation was introduced in Chapter 3. It can be measured by estimating the amount of time the processor is busy within a time interval x and dividing that by x. The process that would normally be running on the transputer (the $main$) is run as the high-priority process of a PRI PAR. The low-priority process is the $supervisor$:

```
PRI PAR
    main ()
    supervisor ()
```

By the definition of the PRI PAR, the $supervisor$ process is only allowed to run if the high-priority process, $main$, is idle. The $supervisor$ simply measures the amount of time it is allowed to run, *idle*, and at the end of a sufficiently long time interval x, it computes the processor utilisation as $((x-idle)/x)$. The utilisation measurement resulted in the following utilisation figures:

process	utilisation
renderer	0.07
splitter	0.98.

The above figures indicate that we have managed to relieve the renderer from the largest part of the work which does not require the use of the processor array. The performance of our system can be improved by employing several splitting transputers, each splitting a different polygon. According to the above figures, 14 splitters would be required in order to balance the performance of the renderer.

Notice that we used the definition of processor utilisation as the fraction of time that the processor is engaged in useful computation because our objective was to compare the work load of the renderer to that of the splitter rather than determining the speedup over a uniprocessor.

The splitters can be arranged and connected to the links of the renderer in a number of ways among which are the following:

1. Tree

The splitters are arranged as a tree and connected to the 4 links of the renderer. In this way the bandwidth of all 4 links of the renderer can be utilised. The internal nodes of the tree will be burdened with the additional task of copying messages from their children nodes to their parents. To avoid this potential bottleneck, merger transputers can be employed (figure 5.7).

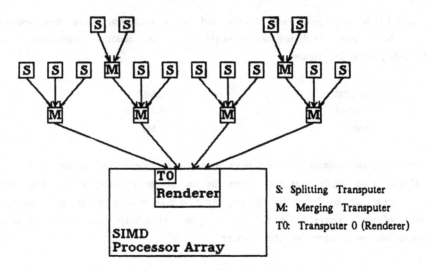

Figure 5.7. A 14-splitter tree with mergers

When mergers are used, the splitters only appear at the leafs of the tree. The merger could be defined in Occam as follows:

```
PROC merge ([]CHAN in, CHAN out)
    VAL max.buff IS
    VAL buff.0    IS    0:
    VAL buff.1    IS    1:
    [2] [max.buff] BYTE buff:
    [2] INT buff.length:
    INT buff.ind:

    ...PROC input.to.buff.alt (VAL INT buff.id, INT length)
        --input.to.buff.alt is defined below
    ...PROC output.from.buff (VAL INT buff.id, length)

    SEQ
        buff.ind := 0
        input.to.buff.alt (buff.0, buff.length[buff.0])
```

```
WHILE  TRUE
    IF
        (buff.ind  =  buff.0)
            SEQ
                PAR
                    input.to.buff.alt  (buff.1,  buff.length[buff.1])
                    output.from.buff  (buff.0,  buff.length[buff.0])
                buff.ind  :=  buff.1
        TRUE
            SEQ
                PAR
                    input.to.buff.alt  (buff.0,  buff.length[buff.0])
                    output.from.buff  (buff.1,  buff.length[buff.1])
                buff.ind  :=  buff.0
    :
```

where $input.to.buff.alt$ is defined as:

```
PROC  input.to.buff.alt  (VAL  INT  buff.id,  INT  length)
    BYTE  length.byte:
    ALT  i  =  0  FOR  (SIZE  in)
        in[i]  ?  length.byte
            SEQ
                length  :=  INT  (length.byte)
                in[i]  ?  [buff  [buff.id]  FROM  0  FOR  length]
    :
```

The $input.to.buff$ process of the renderer would also have to be changed in order to
cater for input from 4 channels. The input process defined above could be used.

2. Pipeline

The splitters are connected in a pipeline (figure 5.8). Each splitter copies the output of all
previous splitters in the pipeline to its successor. The pipeline arrangement is convenient for
the implementation of a hidden surface elimination method which will be described in §5.4.2.

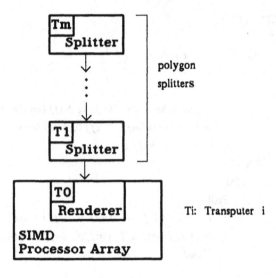

Figure 5.8. A pipeline of splitters

5.3.3. Communication Cost

It can be seen from the communication protocol defined in §5.2.1 that the number of bytes required for a polygon description in terms of precomputed surface patches is $3*s + w + 5$. 5 bytes are required for the extent information and the colour of the polygon, the w bytes are made up by the *prev.window.coverage* value of each window in the extent and 3 bytes are needed for each of the s patch descriptions. If we assume that the average values of w and s are 5 and 10 respectively, then 40 bytes are required for one polygon description.

The polygon descriptions must be transmitted from the splitters to the renderer via a transputer link. If array slice communication is used and link comunications are kept as independent as possible from the processing task by the use of buffering, as we discussed in §5.2.2, a maximum link data rate of 0.5 Mbytes / sec can be achieved. This data rate allows for the transmission of about 12,000 polygon descriptions / sec. If a greater data rate is required, the other 3 links of the renderer can also be utilised.

5.4. Hidden Surface Elimination on the Disputer

We shall now describe two approaches for eliminating the hidden surfaces (HSE). The first is an image space approach and is handled by the processor array. The second approach operates in object space and is handled by the splitters.

5.4.1. Hidden Surface Elimination on the Processor Array

The depth of the polygon's plane at each of the pixels it covers is computed incrementally from window to window and the z-buffer algorithm is used. This approach was described in detail in §3.3. The communication protocol of §5.2.1 must be modified to include the coefficients of the polygon's plane equation a, b and c:

$$\begin{aligned}
\text{POLYGON} ::= \ &extent.xmin_1 \ extent.ymin_1 \\
&extent.xlength_1 \ extent.ylength_1 \ colour_1 \\
&a_2 \ b_2 \ c_2 \\
&\{ \text{SUB.POLYGON} \}^{extent.xlength \ \times \ extent.ylength}
\end{aligned}$$

This approach is very general; it can correctly eliminate the hidden surfaces from models which consist of touching or even penetrating polygons. However a large memory, the size of the frame buffer, is required for the z-buffer. The processor array cost of the combined filling and HSE operations if the z-buffer algorithm is used, will be:

$$T''_{\text{FILL,HSE}} = T''_{\text{FILL}} + T_{\text{HSE}}$$

where T''_{FILL} and T_{HSE} were introduced in §5.3.1 and §3.3 respectively. Of course, $T''_{\text{FILL,HSE}} < T_{\text{FILL,HSE}}$ because, for most values of the performance variables, $T''_{\text{FILL}} < T_{\text{FILL}}$.

The evaluation of the linear function required for the z-buffer algorithm is expensive if a bit-serial processor array is being used. We shall next describe a method of performing the HSE at no cost at all to the processor array, i.e. $T''_{\text{FILL,HSE}} = T''_{\text{FILL}}$, and only a modest cost to the splitters.

5.4.2. Hidden Surface Elimination on a Transputer Pipeline

As we mentioned in §5.3.2, one of the ways of connecting the splitters is a pipeline (figure 5.8). This configuration can be used to implement an HSE algorithm.

The renderer receives from the pipeline of splitters a sequence of polygon descriptions. The polygons are rendered in the order of arrival of their descriptions. Thus if two polygons overlap, the visible polygon will be the one whose polygon description arrived last since it will overwrite the previous one in the area of overlap. If the descriptions are ordered back-to-front (i.e. the description of the polygon that is the furthest away from the view point arrives first), the HSE problem is solved. This is the painter's algorithm and was described in §1.3.2. Notice that it is not always possible to order a set of polygons back-to-front. Figure 5.9 gives two examples of polygons that cannot be ordered in this manner.

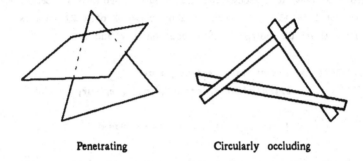

Penetrating   Circularly occluding

Figure 5.9. Two cases of polygons that cannot be ordered back-to-front

In order to be able to order the polygons we need an unambiguous measure of distance which will serve as the "ordering key". It must be unambiguous in the sense that if $d1$, the measure of distance of polygon $P1$, is less than $d2$, the measure of distance of polygon $P2$, then $P1$ is always the visible polygon in the area of overlap of $P1$ and $P2$ in the (X_s, Y_s) screen coordinate system (if such an area of overlap exists). Two obvious candidate measures of distance are:

    1. The distance in eye coordinates of an arbitrary vertex of a polygon (x_e, y_e, z_e) from the view point (called the *true* distance). If the view point is at the origin, true distance can be calculated as:

$$d = \sqrt{(x_e^2 + y_e^2 + z_e^2)}.$$

    2. The z_e eye coordinate of an arbitrary vertex of a polygon.

Neither of the above distance measures is unambiguous unless the polygonal model is constrained by certain *well-spacedness* rules. Willis has investigated these rules for both of the above distance measures [Will77, Will78]. For each distance measure Willis derived a *proximity boundary* which is an area around a polygon. If no polygon lies in the proximity boundary of another polygon, well-spacedness is satisfied and the relevant distance measure is unambiguous. The proximity boundaries for the above two distance measures are illustrated in figure 5.10 for the simpler 2D case when the polygon is a line segment L.

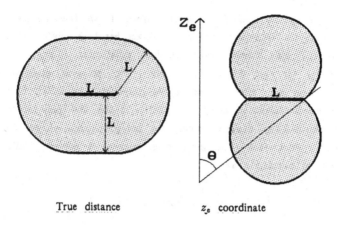

True distance z_e coordinate

Figure 5.10. Proximity boundaries

The true distance measure is more expensive to compute than the z_e distance measure (the former requires 3 multiplications and 1 square root calculation). On the other hand, the area within the proximity boundary of a polygon when the z_e distance measure is used, will be dependant on the maximum angle, Θ, subtended by a point on the polygon and the Z_e axis (figure 5.10). The larger Θ is, the greater the area within the proximity boundary. The maximum value of Θ is, however, restricted if clipping is used. The angle between the Z_e axis and one of the edges of the clipping pyramid (see figure 1.3) is the maximum possible value of Θ. If clipping is not performed, the z_e distance measure should not be used because the proximity boundaries of polygons will contain excessively large areas since Θ will be unrestricted.

When a polygon is subdivided, the sum of the proximity boundaries of the subdivisions is smaller than the proximity boundary of the original polygon [Will78]. It is therefore possible to transform an arbitrary polygonal model so that it is well-spaced provided that there are no touching polygons in the model. This is done once only during a preprocessing stage. The polygonal model is thus restricted to be *still* i.e. polygons are not allowed to move relative to each other at run-time; only the view point can be changed. Still models are useful, for example, in modelling the terrain of a flight simulator.

We have mentioned above that touching polygons are disallowed because a model containing such polygons cannot be transformed into a well-spaced model. However touching polygons that belong to the same *convex* 3D object (e.g. a cube) can be treated as a special case. The polygons that make up a 3D convex object can be divided into 2 sets. The first set contains those polygons that are visible from the view point, the second those that are not visible i.e. are facing away from the view point. The polygons that are facing away from the view point are the *back faces* of the object. If we eliminate the back faces of a convex object then the HSE problem for that object has been solved because front faces of the same convex object cannot possibly occlude each other. The back faces can be identified by checking the sign of the c coefficient of the polygons' plane equations in the screen coordinate system (i.e. after the perspective projection). In a left handed coordinate system with the viewing direction along the positive z-axis and polygon vertices defined according to an anticlockwise traversal around the polygon (when viewed from its visible side), $c < 0$ implies a back face. The screen coordinates of 3 polygon vertices, (x_i, y_i) | $i:1..3$, can be used to calculate c as:

$$c = x_1(y_2-y_3) + x_2(y_3-y_1) + x_3(y_1-y_2).$$

The sign of c can also be regarded as a test on the order of the 3 vertices (clockwise or anticlockwise). Back face elimination will typically halve the number of polygons that require further HSE consideration in a model consisting of convex objects only. The HSE problem for the rest of the polygons can then be solved by ordering the polygons according to distance from the view point and using the painter's algorithm as described above.

It is now easy to see how the above ideas can be implemented on the pipeline of splitters. Each splitter is assigned a polygon. After applying the viewing transformation (see §5.5) and projecting into screen coordinates, a splitter determines whether its polygon is a back face. If it is, the splitter does not proceed to the construction of the polygon description but simply copies polygon descriptions from its predecessor to its successor for the rest of the current frame. If its polygon is not a back face however, the splitter divides it into subwindow polygons and thus constructs the polygon description. It then uses the distance measure (e.g. the z_e coordinate of one of its polygon's vertices) in order to place the polygon description at the correct position in the ordered sequence of polygon descriptions that travel through the pipeline. The distance measure must therefore be included in the polygon description:

$$\text{POLYGON} ::= distance_2\ extent.xmin_1\ extent.ymin_1$$
$$extent.xlength_1\ extent.ylength_1\ colour_1$$
$$\{\ \text{SUB.POLYGON}\ \}^{extent.xlength\ \times\ extent.ylength}$$

The Occam definition of the splitter (§5.2.3) must now be altered so that the splitter can become part of a pipeline of splitters that implement HSE as described in this section:

```
PROC split (CHAN in, out)
  ...PROC split.to.buff (VAL INT buff.id, INT buff.ptr)
  ...PROC output.from.buff (VAL INT buff.id, length)
  ...PROC input.to.buff (VAL INT buff.id, INT length)


  VAL max.buff   IS
  VAL buff.0     IS   0:
  VAL buff.1     IS   1:
  [2] [max.buff] BYTE buff:
  [2] INT buff.length:


  SEQ
    ...initialisations
    WHILE TRUE   --for each frame
      SEQ
        ...apply viewing and perspective transformations
        ...calculate c coefficient of polygon's plane

        IF
          (c < 0)
            ...copy polygon descriptions from input to output until
                              --next.frame value is found
          TRUE
            SEQ
              split.to.buff (buff.0, buff.length[buff.0])
              ...calculate distance measure
              ...copy polygon descriptions from input to output
                --until either next.frame value is found or
                --distance.measure.of.input.polygon
                --  < distance.measure.of.local.polygon
              --output local polygon description
              output.from.buff (buff.0, buff.length[buff.0])
              ...copy polygon descriptions from input to output until
                --next.frame value is found (if not already found)

    :
```

The communication protocol of §5.2.1 must now be extended. Polygon descriptions belonging to the same frame are grouped together to make up a frame description. Frame descriptions are separated by a special value, *next.frame*. The viewing transformation parameters follow the next.frame value:

$$\text{FRAME} ::= \textit{next.frame}_1 \text{ VIEWING.PARAMETERS}$$
$$\{\textit{next.polygon}_1 \text{ POLYGON}\}^*$$

It is not necessary to have one transputer for the splitter process of every polygon in the model. The splitter processes of more than one polygon can be pipelined within each transputer. For example, if 14 splitting transputers are required to match the performance of the rendering transputer (see §5.3.2), the splitter processes for all the polygons in the model may be distributed among these 14 transputers. Here, the flexibility of Occam in distributing processes among one or more transputers becomes apparent.

Notice that HSE could be implemented on the splitter tree described in §5.3.2 if the mergers were altered so as to copy polygon descriptions in order of their distance measures. One problem with the tree of splitters (when compared to the pipeline of splitters) is that it is harder to broadcast the viewing transformation parameters for each frame to the splitters. A possible solution would be to broadcast the viewing transformation parameters for each frame from the root of the tree of splitters.

To summarise, in this section we have described a way of performing the HSE operation in the pipeline of splitters. At the expense of some preprocessing, HSE is performed at the cost of no more than P comparisons per splitter process plus the cost of determining the distance measure, where P is the number of polygons in the model. The determination of the distance measure will require no computation at all if z_e is used as the distance measure. The cost to the processor array is nil i.e. $T''_{\text{FILL,HSE}} = T''_{\text{FILL}}$. Only still models can be handled and touching polygons are only allowed if they belong to the same convex object.

5.5. Further Extensions of the Renderer / Splitter System

We have described in this Chapter how the Disputer (a system constructed out of a processor array with a transputer controller and a transputer network), can improve on the polygon rendering performance of the methods described in Chapters 3 and 4 which only use the processor array. This Chapter has so far been concerned with the fundamental rendering operations of filling and HSE.

It is easy to extend the renderer / splitter system in order to provide smooth shading, by incrementally evaluating bivariate linear shading functions for each polygon on the processor array in the manner described in §3.4.2. The coefficients of the linear shading functions for each polygon must be determined by the relevant splitter and passed to the renderer by extending the communication protocol as we did in §5.4.1 for the coefficients of the HSE function.

The function of the splitter can easily be extended to provide object space operations on its polygon. For each new frame, a splitter receives the new viewing transformation parameters, applies them to the coordinates of its polygon, it then clips its polygon against the 3D clipping pyramid (see Chapter 1) and finally projects the polygon onto the plane of the screen (perspective transformation). All of the above transformations take place before splitting the polygon into subwindow polygons. The viewing transformation parameters can easily be broadcast if the splitters are connected in a pipeline.

Another extension of the renderer / splitter system is the implementation of a concave to convex polygon decomposition algorithm. This would allow the inclusion of concave polygons in the model. A variety of algorithms exist for this purpose, see for example [Gree83].

Finally, a limited form of anti-aliasing can be accomodated by anti-aliasing the precomputed surface patches as described in Chapter 4.

Of course any extensions to the renderer or splitter will invalidate the utilisation figures of §5.3.2 and new figures will have to be estimated in order to determine how many splitting transputers to use.

5.6. Conclusion

A network of MIMD transputers can significantly improve the performance of rendering operations on a SIMD processor array, by off-loading the controller of the processor array from the largest part of the sequential (non-SIMD) code. The transputers construct compact descriptions of convex polygons in terms of surface patches which they send to the processor array; the latter uses precomputed surface patches in order to fill the polygons in the frame buffer. High bandwidth results (polygon filling with surface patches) are thus achieved by low bandwidth communication (transmission of surface patch descriptions). The operation of HSE can also be handled by the transputer network at the cost of some modest restrictions on the polygonal model. Even if of little current practical importance (not everyone has a Disputer yet!) the work presented in this Chapter is an example of programming a dual-paradigm parallel processor and a demonstration of necessary techniques (treatment of the SIMD processor array as a special node of the MIMD network, programming the whole machine in an extension of the MIMD programming language, off-loading the sequential code from the controller of the SIMD processor array and keeping the communication between the MIMD and the SIMD parts low).

Chapter 6
Control Parallel Versus Data Parallel Polygon Clipping

6.1. Introduction

The INMOS transputer and the AMT DAP (see Chapter 2) are two very different examples of a general purpose parallel processor. They lie at opposite ends of the spectrum that defines the distribution of processing power and the organisation of control; the former offers coarse grain control parallelism and the latter fine grain data parallelism. It is therefore likely that the application areas in which the two machines can be efficiently employed are different (although they certainly overlap).

Can we define the application areas in which each of the two machines can be employed efficiently? Is it possible to decide which machine can provide better performance for a particular task without implementing the task on both machines? Would it be possible to compare the cost-effectiveness of the two machines for the same task? (Notice that the last question is more relevant now that both machines are commercially available).

The above questions are not easy to quantify but they are very interesting because they are relevant not only to the transputer and the DAP, but to the whole class of MIMD and SIMD parallel processors.

This Chapter was originally intended to provide the answers to all of the above questions but after a significant amount of wasted effort and paper it was realised that the answers to the above questions involve variables whose values are algorithm dependent and can not usually be predicted. Thus, this Chapter merely attempts to compare the two parallel processors in the very restricted case of the graphics operation of polygon clipping. It is nevertheless possible to learn some lessons about the more general case from this restricted comparison which, incidentally, resulted in a novel SIMD implementation of the polygon clipping operation.

6.2. Estimating Performance

The simple metric of Millions of Instructions Per Second (MIPS) is very misleading as an indication of the performance of a parallel machine not only because the definition of an "instruction" is a debatable issue, but also because it says nothing about the portion of these MIPS that can be usefully exploited by a particular task.

The concept of processor utilisation is only applicable to parallel processing; in sequential processing problems such as synchronisation delays, communication overheads and imperfect assignement of data to processors do not arise. Let us define the processor utilisation as the fraction of time that a processor is engaged in useful computation. If we know the processor utilisation (pu) of the implementation of a task on a parallel processor which offers $mips$ MIPS (assuming that we have an acceptable definiton of an "instruction"), then we may think that we can express the expected performance as:

$$performance = mips \times pu \qquad | \qquad pu: 0..1$$

However the above metric can also be misleading because there are many algorithms for solving a problem some of which require more computation than others. It is possible that algorithm A gives a lower value to the above performance metric than algorithm B, but A executes faster than B because it has much lower complexity. Let us see an example. Consider the evaluation of a linear function over the "initial" window presented in Chapter 3. We described a method which can perform the evaluation at a cost of $2\log_2 N$ planar additions. The processor utilisation is 0.5 because any one of the $2\log_2 N$ planar additions is only performed on half the points of the $N{\times}N$ grid (see the masks of figure 3.3). Now consider the following method for the initial evaluation of the linear function $F(x,y)=ax+by+c$. The value of F is computed for the coordinates of the window (xw, yw) and broadcast to create a planar number R. Then the constant planar integer $[a]$ is added to R N-1 times using conditional planar additions. The mask, Q, for conditional planar addition $k: 1..N$-1 is defined as:

$$Q(i,j) = \text{TRUE}, \ i \geqslant k$$
$$= \text{FALSE}, \ i < k$$

where i is the column index. In other words Q has its $N-k$ rightmost columns set to TRUE. In a similar way $[b]$ is added to R using N-1 conditional planar addtions with masks which are equivalent to the masks defined above rotated by 90^0 anticlockwise. It is not hard to prove that the processor utilisation is 0.5 for the method just described. However its cost is $2(N$-1) planar additions (as opposed to $2\log_2 N$ planar additions of the previous method).

The above example illustrates the fact that the complexity (c) of the algorithm used must be taken into account in the calculation of the performance metric. Complexity is here defined as the total amount of computation that the algorithm performs. A better performance metric is then the following:

$$performance = mips * pu / c$$

where c is expressed in Millions of Instructions (MI's). Cost-effectiveness can be defined as the ratio of performance over the price of the relevant parallel processor. The problem then that we face when trying to compare the performance of two different parallel processors for a particular task is the absence of proven optimal algorithms for the task on each parallel processor. We define the optimal algorithm to be the one that maximises the value of the performance metric for a given task and parallel processor.

Even if the optimal algorithms are known, the above performance metric is only useful for very rough estimations of performance because the values of pu and c can not be predicted accurately.

In the following sections we have derived the performance of the polygon clipping operation on transputers and the DAP by employing the "stopwatch" method i.e. by timing the two implementations. We have avoided the search for optimal algorithms for each of the two parallel processors by extracting control and data parallelism out of the same sequential polygon clipping algorithm. Thus the complexity of both parallel implementations is the same.

6.3.   The Sutherland-Hodgman Polygon Clipping Algorithm

The objective of the clipping operation is to discard those primitives (or parts of them) that do not lie within a certain clipping volume of eye coordinate object space, as described in Chapter 1. The clipping volume usually takes the form of the truncated pyramid shown in figure 1.3. The most common modelling primitive in high performance graphics systems is the planar polygon and efficient polygon clipping algorithms are therefore necessary. It is not possible to clip a polygon by clipping each of its edges independently because the result will not necessarily be a *closed* polygon and will therefore not be suitable for filling. Special polygon clipping algorithms are therefore necessary.

The Sutherland-Hodgman polygon clipping algorithm has found wide application due to its simplicity and generality and is best described in their paper [Suth74b]. In this section we discuss the key concepts involved in the algorithm which are essential for the explanation of the parallel approaches to its implementation presented in §6.4 and §6.5. The polygon to be clipped is represented as a sequence of vertices which occur in the order dictated by an anticlockwise traversal around the polygon. The polygon is clipped against (the *clipping plane* defined by) the first face of the clipping pyramid and a new sequence of vertices is produced which represents the polygon clipped against the first face of the pyramid. The process is repeated for each of the six faces of the clipping pyramid. The sequence of vertices that are produced by the last clipping stage, represents the polygon clipped against the clipping pyramid. Figure 6.1 demonstrates the process.

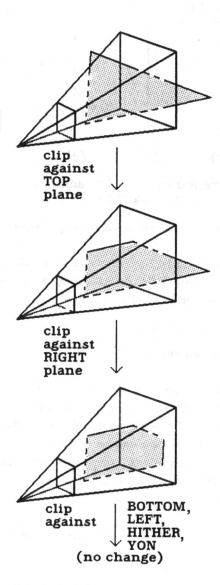

clip
against
TOP
plane

clip
against
RIGHT
plane

clip   BOTTOM,
against   LEFT,
          HITHER,
          YON
(no change)

Figure 6.1.   The Sutherland-Hodgman polygon clipping algorithm

116

Clipping against a single clipping plane is performed by considering the polygon's vertices in pairs (v_i, v_{i+1}). For each such pair 0,1 or 2 vertices are appended to the clipped polygon sequence, depending on the relationship of the vertex pair to the clipping plane. The 4 possible cases are demonstrated in figure 6.2. Note that the first vertex of the polygon must also be repeated as the last.

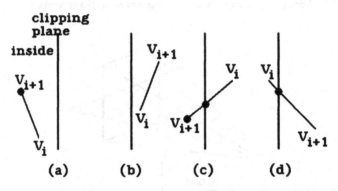

$\bullet$ **represent vertices added to the clipped polygon sequence**

Figure 6.2. Clipping against a single clipping plane.

The next subsection describes how the key calculations of determining the relationship between a vertex and a clipping plane and calculating the intersection of a clipping plane with a line segment can be performed efficiently.

6.3.1. Key Clipping Calculations

As mentioned in Chapter 1, clipping is performed in the eye coordinate system. Let us assume that eye coordinates are homogeneous i.e. the point (x_e, y_e, z_e) is represented as a quadruplet $(w_e x_e, w_e y_e, w_e z_e, w_e)$ for $w_e \neq 0$, see [Fole83] §7.2. The advantage of homogeneous coordinates is that they allow the transformation matrix for translation to be combined with other transformation matrices using matrix multiplication rather than addition. Thus all the basic transformations (rotation, translation, scaling, shearing) can be combined in a consistent manner i.e. by matrix multiplication.

Consider the YZ projection of the part of the clipping pyramid that lies above the $y=0$ plane shown in figure 6.3.

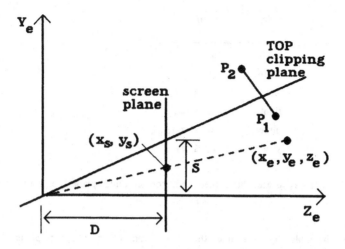

Figure 6.3. YZ projection of (part of) the clipping pyramid

The perspective projection of a point (x_e, y_e, z_e) onto the screen plane is:

$$(x_s, y_s) = (Dx_e/z_e, \ Dy_e/z_e)$$

and this can be converted into a dimensionless fraction by dividing by S:

$$(x_s, y_s) = ((D/S)x_e/z_e, \ (D/S)y_e/z_e)$$

where $-1 \le x_s, y_s \le 1$. (The dimensionless fraction is particularly useful if the different screen coordinate systems of several display devices have to be catered for).

A point (x_e, y_e, z_e) is within the top clipping plane if $y_s \le 1$ or $y_e \le (S/D) z_e$ (z_e can be assumed to be positive if we perform hither clipping). The bottom, left and right clipping planes can be treated in a similar way. Thus if the viewing transformation calculates the w_e coordinate of a point (x_e, y_e, z_e) as $w_e = (S/D) z_e$, then the tests for a point being inside each of the six clipping planes are the following:

inside	if
top	$y_e \leq w_e$
bottom	$y_e \geq -w_e$
left	$x_e \geq -w_e$
right	$x_e \leq w_e$
hither	$z_e \geq z_{\mathrm{HITHER}}$
yon	$z_e \leq z_{\mathrm{YON}}$

where $z = z_{\mathrm{HITHER}}$ and $z = z_{\mathrm{YON}}$ are the hither and yon clipping planes respectively (see figure 1.3).

We also need to be able to determine the intersection of a clipping plane with a line segment whose two endpoints lie on either side of the clipping plane. We use the method suggested in [Suth74b]. Consider the points $P_1 = (x_{e1}, y_{e1}, z_{e1})$ and $P_2 = (x_{e2}, y_{e2}, z_{e2})$ lying on either side of the top clipping plane in figure 6.3. The parametric equations of the line segment from P_1 to P_2 can be written as:

$$x_e = x_{e1} + \alpha(x_{e2} - x_{e1})$$
$$y_e = y_{e1} + \alpha(y_{e2} - y_{e1})$$
$$z_e = z_{e1} + \alpha(z_{e2} - z_{e1})$$

where $0 \leq \alpha \leq 1$. The value of α at the intersection of the line segment P_1-P_2 with the top clipping plane is:

$$\alpha = (y_{e1} - w_{e1}) \, / \, ((y_{e1} - w_{e1}) - (y_{e2} - w_{e2}))$$

and if this value is substituted into the parametric equation of the line segment, we get the coordinates of the intersection. The denominator in the expression for α is guaranteed to be non-zero by the fact that P_1 and P_2 are on opposite sides of the top clipping plane. Intersections with other clipping planes can be found in a similar manner.

6.3.2. Scope for Parallelism

Clipping may not be the performance bottleneck of the graphics output pipeline described in Chapter 1, but it requires a significant amount of computation which necessitates parallel processing especially when complex scenes have to be displayed in real-time or near real-time.

The only restriction that the Sutherland-Hodgman algorithm imposes on the order of clipping, is that a polygon must be clipped sequentially against the 6 clipping planes. In other words a polygon can not be clipped against more than one clipping plane at the same time. There are three main ways of introducing parallelism into the algorithm:

A. Different polygons can be clipped against different clipping planes at the same time, or

B. A large number of polygons can be clipped against the same clipping plane at the same time, or

C. Both A and B.

The first method (A) results in control parallelism and requires a pipeline of 6 clippers, each clipping against a different clipping plane, see §6.4. The second method (B) results in data parallelism and can be implemented on a SIMD processor array as shown in §6.5. We are not aware of any previous SIMD implementations of the Sutherland-Hodgman algorithm (or of any other polygon clipping algorithm). The last method (C) involves both control and data parallelism and could be implemented on a pipeline of SIMD processors! This method will not be considered any further.

6.4. A Control Parallel Implementation of the Sutherland-Hodgman Algorithm

The following control parallel implementation of the Sutherland-Hodgman algorithm is not novel; Clark [Clar82] constructed a pipeline of purpose built VLSI chips (the Geometry Engine) for this purpose and a transputer implementation of the pipeline is reported in [Theo85]. The pipeline implementation of the Sutherland-Hodgman algorithm is presented here for comparison with the data parallel implementation of §6.5.

6.4.1. Description of the Control Parallel Implementation

The Sutherland-Hodgman algorithm can easily be distributed on a pipeline of 6 processors. Each processor is assigned the task of clipping against one of the 6 clipping planes as described in §6.3. Processor i (i: 1..6) receives as input polygons that have been clipped against clipping planes 1..i-1 and clips them against clipping plane i (the first processor receives the unclipped polygons). The resulting polygons, now clipped against clipping planes 1..i, are output to processor i+1 (the last processor outputs polygons which have been clipped against all 6 clipping planes). Figure 6.4 illustrates the pipeline.

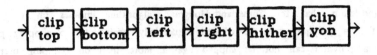

Figure 6.4.   A clipping pipeline

We shall next describe the operation of a single clipping stage, the top one. Two sets of variables are used to store the coordinates of succesive vertices v_1 and v_2:

REAL32 $x1$, $y1$, $z1$, $w1$, $x2$, $y2$, $z2$, $w2$:
BOOL $insidev1$, $insidev2$:

The two Booleans are used to store the relationship of v_1 and v_2 to the clipping plane. For each successive pair of vertices v_1 and v_2, the following actions take place:

1. Determine the relationship of v_1 and v_2 to the (top) clipping plane:

$insidev1 := (y1 \leq w1)$
$insidev2 := (y2 \leq w2)$

Notice that only one of the above two comparisons need take place in each loop iteration.

2. If both vertices are inside the clipping plane, output v_2 to the next clipping stage:

IF
    $(insidev1$ AND $insidev2)$
        ...output v_2

3. If only v_1 is inside the clipping plane, output the intersection of the clipping plane with the edge v_1-v_2 to the next clipping stage:

IF
    $(insidev1$ AND (NOT $insidev2))$
        SEQ
            ...calculate intersection of clipping plane with v_1-v_2
            ...output intersection

4. If only v_2 is inside the clipping plane, output the intersection of the clipping plane with v_1-v_2 followed by v_2 to the next clipping stage:

> IF
>> ((NOT *insidev1*) AND *insidev2*)
>>> SEQ
>>>> ...calculate intersection of clipping plane with v_1-v_2
>>>> ...output intersection
>>>> ...output v_2

5. Finally if neither vertex is inside the clipping plane, no action need take place.

Buffering is used for the transmission of polygon data between clipping stages in order to avoid synchronisation delays. The 5 other clipping stages operate in a similar manner. A process is defined for each of the 6 stages:

> PROC *clip.plane* (CHAN *in*, *out*)
>> ... body

where *in* and *out* are the channels connecting the stage to its predecessor and its successor in the pipeline respectively. The Occam PAR statement and the appropriate channel connections are used to construct the clipping pipeline:

> CHAN $c1$, $c2$, $c3$, $c4$, $c5$, $c6$, $c7$:
> PAR
>> *clip.top* ($c1$, $c2$)
>> *clip.bottom* ($c2$, $c3$)
>> *clip.left* ($c3$, $c4$)
>> *clip.right* ($c4$, $c5$)
>> *clip.hither* ($c5$, $c6$)
>> *clip.yon* ($c6$, $c7$)

(a variant of the PAR statement, the PLACED PAR, is used to place the processes on different transputers). The Occam implementation of one clipping stage is shown in Appendix 2.

6.4.2. Performance of the Control Parallel Implementation

A large number of the polygons that constitute our model will usually lie outside the clipping pyramid. It is therefore reasonable to assume that each of the clipping stages will have to deal with fewer polygons than its predecessors in the pipeline; thus the first clipping stage will determine the rate of flow of polygons through the pipeline i.e. the rate at which polygons are clipped. Let $t_{CLIP.ONE.PLANE}$ represent the cost of clipping one polygon against one clipping plane. The time to clip P polygons against the 6 clipping planes is:

$$T_{CLIP} = (P+6) * t_{CLIP.ONE.PLANE}$$

where $6 * t_{CLIP.ONE.PLANE}$ is the amount of time taken to "fill" the pipeline of 6 clipping stages and it can be ignored if P is sufficiently large. Our INMOS T414 transputer implementation resulted in $t_{CLIP.ONE.PLANE}$ = 0.5ms; about 2,000 polygons can therefore be clipped per second. Notice that the bandwidth of the transputer links is not the performance limiting factor in this case provided that buffering is used between stages to avoid synchronisation delays. Assuming that a polygon requires 100 bytes (each vertex consists of four 4-byte coordinates), the 2,000 polygons/s require a data rate of 200 Kbytes/s which is significantly less than the bandwidth of a transputer link.

The T800 floating point transputer should provide better performance since real arithmetic calculations are used in clipping.

6.5. A Data Parallel Implementation of the Sutherland-Hodgman Algorithm

In this section we shall describe how the Sutherland-Hodgman polygon clipping algorithm can be implemented on a SIMD processor array. Our particular implementation is based on the DAP processor array.

6.5.1. Distribution of the Polygon Vertices

There are two basic ways of distributing the vertices of the polygons to be clipped among the PE's of the processor array:

1. Assign one vertex to each PE.
2. Assign the vertices of one polygon to each PE.

The two methods are demonstrated in figure 6.5.

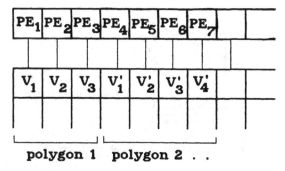

A. Vertex per PE

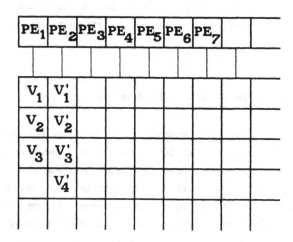

B. Polygon per PE

Figure 6.5. Distributing the vertex data among the PE's.

The first method (1) has two disadvantages; first it requires interprocessor communication in order to access the adjacent vertex data necessary in the Sutherland–Hodgman algorithm. Second, every time a vertex is deleted or a new vertex is created during clipping, it is necessary to shift the whole array of vertices in the appropriate direction in order to close the gap or create space for the new vertex. It is also necessary to perform shifts when the second method is used, but the shifts for a whole "row" of vertices can be performed in parallel. Furthermore, as the number of vertices can increase as well as decrease during clipping, one should start with fewer vertices than the number of PE's if the first method is used. In the worst conceivable case, every edge of every polygon will intersect two clipping planes and the number of vertices will be at least doubled after clipping against all 6 clipping planes, see figure 6.6. Thus we should start with less than $1/2 N^2$ vertices, where N^2 is the number of PE's, and this would result in low processor utilisation because clipping usually reduces, rather than increasing, the number of vertices.

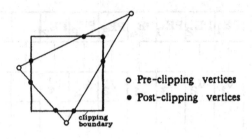

o Pre-clipping vertices
● Post-clipping vertices

Figure 6.6. Clipping can increase the number of vertices

For the above reasons we decided to use the second method of assigning vertices to PE's i.e. assign all the vertices of a polygon to a single PE. A disadvantage of this method is that if there is a wide variance on the number of vertices per polygon, some PE's will be underutilised.

6.5.2. Description of the Data Parallel Implementation

The data parallel polygon clipper was implemented on the 64×64 ICL DAP processor array using DAP Fortran [ICL80, ICL81] but, for consistency with the rest of this book, we shall present it in Occam with the planar data type extensions descussed in Chapter 2. However, before describing the details of the implementation we shall give a high level pseudo-code description in order to clarify the algorithm. In the following piece of pseudo-code variable names are in lower case. The PAR statement signifies parallel execution:

```
FOR c := 0 TO 5     { There are 6 clipping planes }
    FOR v := 0 TO maximum_number_of_vertices_in_any_polygon - 1
        PAR p := 0 TO N²-1  { There are N² polygons (one per PE) }
            insidev1(p)  := INSIDE(clipping_plane(c), vertex(p,v))
            insidev2(p)  := INSIDE(clipping_plane(c), vertex(p,v+1))
            intersection(p)  := FIND_INTERSECTION(clipping_plane(c),
                                    EDGE(vertex(p,v), vertex(p,v+1)))
            IF (NOT insidev1(p)) AND (NOT insidev2(p)) THEN DELETE(vertex(p,v))
            IF (NOT insidev1(p)) AND insidev2(p) THEN vertex(p,v) := intersection(p)
            IF insidev1(p) AND (NOT insidev2(p))
                THEN INSERT(intersection(p), BETWEEN(vertex(p,v), vertex(p,v+1)))
```

Insertions and deletions do not actually take place immediately but are batched up and processed between successive executions of the outer loop (which steps through the clipping planes).

We shall next describe the details of the algorithm in Occam. The vertices of the N^2 polygons to be clipped are stored in 4 arrays of planar reals (planar integers with suitable scaling could have been used instead). A planar integer is used to store the number of vertices in each polygon:

[max]PLANAR.REAL32 *vertexx, vertexy, vertexz, vertexw*:
PLANAR.INT *n*:

(*max* represents the maximum number of vertices that a polygon is allowed to have). Four arrays of planar reals are necessary for the temporary storage of intersection vertices created during clipping and an array of planar Booleans is used to indicate the positions at which new vertices must be inserted. Two planar Booleans are needed for the storage of the relationship between pairs of vertices from each of the N^2 polygons and the clipping plane:

[max]PLANAR.REAL32 *intersectionx, intersectiony,*
                         intersectionz, intersectionw:
PLANAR.REAL32 *alpha*:   --used in the intersection calculation
[max]PLANAR.BOOL *extravertex*:
PLANAR.BOOL *insidev1, insidev2, mask*:

Initially, the first vertex of every polygon is duplicated as its last vertex and the following 3 steps take place for every *i*:0..*maxvertex*-1 where *maxvertex* represents the number of vertices in the polygon with the largest number of vertices:

1. Determine the relationship between vertices v_i and v_{i+1} of every polygon and the clipping plane:

    insidev1 := *vertexy*[i] $\leq$ *vertexw*[i]
    insidev2 := *vertexy*[i+1] $\leq$ *vertexw*[i+1]

This calculation is shown in §6.3.1. Notice that the same operation is performed for all N^2 polygons in parallel.

2. Calculate the intersection of the edge v_i-v_{i+1} of every polygon with the (top) clipping plane:

$$alpha := (vertexy[i] - vertexw[i]) /$$
$$((vertexy[i] - vertexw[i]) - (vertexy[i+1] - vertexw[i+1]))$$
$$intersectionx[i] := vertexx[i] + (alpha * (vertexx[i+1] - vertexx[i]))$$
$$intersectiony[i] := vertexy[i] + (alpha * (vertexy[i+1] - vertexy[i]))$$
$$intersectionz[i] := vertexz[i] + (alpha * (vertexz[i+1] - vertexz[i]))$$
$$intersectionw[i] := intersectionz[i] * PLANAR.REAL32 (S/D)$$

where S and D are the scalar constants described in §6.3.1. The intersection calculation is performed in parallel for the N^2 polygons although it is not useful for all of them. The denominator in the expression for $alpha$ may be zero for some elements but the error produced in these elements should be ignored because the result of the intersection calculation will not be used in these elements; if the v_i and v_{i+1} vertices of a polygon are on opposite sides of the clipping plane, then the value of the denominator in the expression for $alpha$ will not be zero in the relevant element.

3. Each of the N^2 vertex pairs (v_i, v_{i+1}) must now be classified according to one of the 4 cases of figure 6.2. The classification produces planar Boolean masks which are used in order to take a different action for the vertex pairs that belong to each of the 4 categories. Each of the 4 actions is implemented in parallel for all the vertex pairs of the respective category. The simplest action is taken if both v_i and v_{i+1} are inside the clipping plane (figure 6.2(a)); nothing is done in this case! If both v_i and v_{i+1} are outside the clipping plane (figure 6.2(b)), vertex v_i can be deleted. To this effect, one of the coordinates of v_i is replaced by a special value:

$$mask := (NOT insidev1) AND (NOT insidev2)$$
$$vertexx[i](mask) := PLANAR.REAL32 (DELETE)$$

Two more cases remain to be dealt with. If v_i is outside and v_{i+1} is inside the clipping plane (figure 6.2(c)), then v_i can be replaced by the intersection of edge v_i-v_{i+1} and the clipping plane:

$$mask := (NOT insidev1) AND insidev2$$
$$vertexx[i](mask) := intersectionx[i]$$
$$vertexy[i](mask) := intersectiony[i]$$
$$vertexz[i](mask) := intersectionz[i]$$
$$vertexw[i](mask) := intersectionw[i]$$

Finally, if v_i is inside and v_{i+1} is outside the clipping plane (figure 6.2(d)), the relevant polygon has grown by one extra vertex, the intersection vertex, which must be inserted between v_i and v_{i+1}. Note that the new vertex can not replace v_{i+1} because v_{i+1} may be replaced by a "case 6.2(c)" intersection vertex when (v_{i+1}, v_{i+2}) is considered. The position at which the new vertex has to be inserted must therefore be remembered for later use:

$$extravertex[i] := insidev1 \text{ AND (NOT } insidev2)$$

After performing the above 3 steps for $i:0..maxvertex-1$, all the edges of all the N^2 polygons have been clipped against the (top) clipping plane. Before clipping against the next clipping plane it is necessary to create space for the new vertices produced in "case 6.2(d)" and remove the vertices marked for deletion. $extravertex[i]$ is a planar Boolean that indicates which "columns" of the vertex arrays must be shifted by one place starting from "row" $i+1$ in order to create space for the insertion of new vertices (column here refers to the vertices of a single polygon which reside within the memory of a single PE while row refers to a slice consisting of the ith vertex of every polygon, see figure 6.7b). Note that the data shifting is performed in parallel for all the columns indicated by $extravertex[i]$. Removal of the vertices marked for deletion is carried out in a similar manner. Figure 6.7b illustrates graphically the action of the data parallel polygon clipper for the polygons of figure 6.7a. The DAP Fortran implementation is presented in Appendix 3.

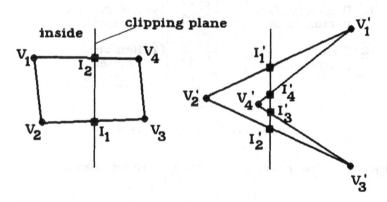

Figure 6.7a. Data parallel polygon clipping – example polygons

128

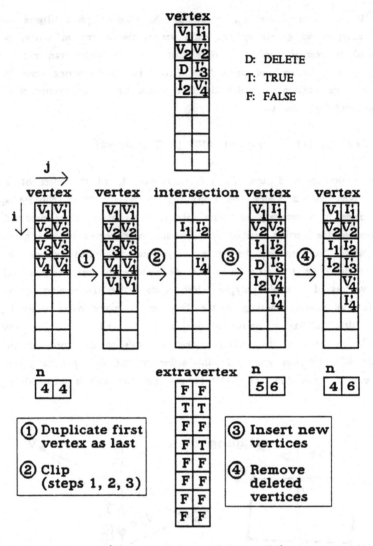

(Dimension j processed in parallel)

Figure 6.7b. Data parallel polygon clipping - example execution

6.5.3. Performance of the Data Parallel Implementation

The data parallel clipper described in the previous section can clip N^2 polygons against one clipping plane in parallel; let $t'_{\text{CLIP.ONE.PLANE}}$ stand for the amount of time taken to execute it. In 3D clipping we usually have to clip against 6 clipping planes (the truncated pyramid of figure 1.3) and thus the clipper has to be executed 6 times in succession. The resulting vertex arrays from each execution will be the input to the next. The time to clip P polygons against 6 clipping planes will therefore be:

$$T'_{\text{CLIP}} = 6 * \lceil P/N^2 \rceil * t'_{\text{CLIP.ONE.PLANE}} .$$

Our implementation on the 64×64 ICL DAP processor array gave $t'_{\text{CLIP.ONE.PLANE}}$ = 25ms. The performance of the implementation can be improved by programming the DAP in assembler rather than DAP Fortran. Also the DAP used was built in the late 1970's and has a cycle time of 200ns. Nevertheless, about 25,000 polygons can be clipped per second using the current implementation.

The data parallel clipper described above uses polygon data that has been distributed to the memories of the DAP PE's. The cost of distributing and retrieving polygon data from the DAP store can be ignored if the clipping operation is part of a data parallel implementation of the graphics output pipeline.

6.5.4. Usefulness of the Data Parallel Implementation

The data parallel clipper can be used in conjunction with data parallel implementations of coordinate transformations and shading calculations in order to provide an efficient data parallel implementation of the non-rendering stages of the graphics output pipeline. The viewing and perspective transformations can trivially be implemented on a SIMD processor array if the vertex data are distributed among the PE's in the manner described in §6.5.1 (polygon per PE). Shading calculations involve the computation of the normal to each polygon, the averaging of the surface normals for all polygons that have a common vertex in order to compute vertex normals and the use of a shading model to calculate vertex intensities from the vertex normals (if the Gouraud shading model is used), see §1.3.3. The surface normal calculation requires the coordinates of the polygons' vertices as input and can be done data parallel since the calculation is the same for all polygons. Similarly the vertex intensity calculation can be performed data parallel once the vertex normals are known. However the calculation of the vertex normals by averaging adjacent surface normals will require the transmission of each polygon's surface normal to the PE's where its neighbouring polygons (in the polygonal model) reside. For rigid objects the vertex normals can be precomputed and kept with the vertex coordinates. The same coordinate transformations that are applied to the polygon vertices are then also applied to the vertex normals thus avoiding the communication and averaging of the surface normals at run time.

6.6. Contrasting the Two Parallel Implementations

The code fragments for the implementation of a single clipping stage on a transputer (§6.4.1) and on the DAP (§6.5.2) are quite similar. However in the case of the transputer pipeline, similar code is run on 6 different transputers each clipping a different polygon against a different clipping plane whereas in the case of the DAP, the same code is executed by all N^2 PE's in order to clip N^2 polygons against a single clipping plane in parallel. The DAP can therefore exploit more parallelism since the number of polygons that can be clipped in parallel (P) is potentially much larger than the number of clipping planes that can be processed in parallel (6). Of course it is possible to exploit data parallelism in a MIMD implementation by having a number of clipping pipelines working in parallel or by distributing the polygon data among the transputers each one of which performs all of the 6 clipping stages to its polygons.

Each of the two approaches assumes a certain environment for its effective use. In the case of the clipping pipeline, it is assumed that it is part of a larger pipeline which contains stages for coordinate transformations, rendering etc. In the case of the data parallel clipper it is assumed that it forms only one stage of a data parallel implementation of the graphics output pipeline; otherwise the polygon data distribution and collection costs are excessive. The polygon data has to be distributed among the DAP PE's anyway but it may be possible to do this once and for all by dividing the polygon data base among the memories of the PE's.

We have given some performance figures for the implementations of the polygon clipper on the transputer and the DAP in §6.4.2 and §6.5.3 respectively. Although tempting, it is dangerous to make any direct comparisons between these figures because of large differences in the size, vintage and cost of the two machines.

6.7. Conclusion

A control parallel and a novel data parallel implementation of a polygon clipping algorithm on transputers and the DAP respectively were presented and contrasted. In general it is not easy to compare the performance and cost-effectiveness of a MIMD and SIMD parallel processor for a particular task. There are a number of parameters whose values can not accurately be determined without implementations on both machines (such as the exact value of algorithmic complexity and processor utilisation) and the optimal algorithms for each task and parallel processor are rarely known. Comparisons are further complicated by differences in the size, vintage and cost of the relevant machines.

Chapter 7
Conclusion

7.1. Contribution of this Work

The step that this work represents towards the goal of the "ultimate display" lies along the path of research that seeks to efficiently implement the techniques that have been and are being devised for the production of realistic scenes. A novel way of exploiting incremental computation for the efficient evaluation of linear polynomial functions on a SIMD processor array was developed. Linear function evaluations can be used to implement rendering operations but the applicability of the method is more general. We have shown how precomputation can enhance the performance of the filling operation on a SIMD processor array and how a dual-paradigm (MIMD-SIMD) parallel processor can be used in order to improve on the performance of rendering on a SIMD processor array alone; even if of little current practical importance this is an example of programming such a processor and a demonstration of the necessary techniques. An unsuccessful attempt to devise a model for the accurate comparison of the performance of SIMD and MIMD architectures led to the discovery of a novel, high-performance, SIMD polygon clipper.

The advantages of using general purpose parallel processors rather than special purpose architectures include low development costs (only the software has to be developed) and a large degree of flexibility since the applications are supported in software; users of general purpose parallel processors can reduce their investment in graphics hardware by using algorithms such as those presented here in order to achieve high, if not state-of-the-art, graphics performance. On the cost-effectiveness scale, special purpose graphics architectures are likely to win if the comparison is made solely in the domain of graphics; however the larger the parallel application suite of the user the more attractive general purpose parallel processors will be. The algorithms presented here should also be useful for certain special purpose parallel graphics systems.

7.2. Discussion

The techniques of incremental computation and precomputation have been widely used in graphics. The well-known Bresenham line drawing algorithm [Bres65], for example, uses both techniques. In some cases, these techniques can be employed in order to program parallel processors efficiently.

It is well known that the most efficient (and usually complex) sequential algorithms are not always the best candidates for parallelisation. It is interesting to note that most of the parallel algorithms we presented were based on the simplest sequential algorithms. For example, we used the z-buffer and the painter's algorithm for HSE which are the simplest sequential HSE algorithms.

SIMD processor arrays are well suited to pixel level operations not only because they provide a high frame buffer update bandwidth, but also because they can efficiently support the extremely useful graphics primitive, RasterOp. Higher level operations however, such as those involving floating point arithmetic, or operations that vary across the data set appear to be better suited to coarse grain MIMD parallelism such as that offered by the transputer.

Data parallel (SIMD) programming is relatively easy because one only has to write a sequential program which is executed on many data items in parallel. Such problems as deadlock do not arise in SIMD programming. However, not all tasks are suited to SIMD implementation and a parallel processor which encompasses both the SIMD and MIMD architectures promises to be both easy to program for tasks suitable for SIMD implementations and of very general utility. The MIMD part of such a machine can sometimes be used to relieve the controller of the SIMD part from the code that can not be efficiently executed in SIMD mode. However it is necessary to keep communication costs between the MIMD part and the controller of the SIMD part as low as possible and one way of achieving this is by communicating references to large precomputed data objects rather than communicating the large data objects themselves.

The SIMD part of a dual-paradigm parallel processor can be viewed as a special node of the MIMD part by assigning to it (i.e. to the SIMD part) a controller which is one of the MIMD processors. The whole system can then be programmed in an extension of the MIMD programming language which includes SIMD data types and operations on them; these are only available on the special SIMD node.

Occam is a very convenient means of expressing parallel programming concepts. We saw in Chapter 5 how useful it is to be able to easily alter the assignment of processes to processors and, in particular, to allocate an arbitrary number of processes to each processor. Occam allows us to construct networks of arbitrary connectivity in a simple manner but the existence of predefined, parameterizable networks (such as pipelines, arrays and trees) would allow the parallel programmer to commence his task at a higher level. It is however debatable whether such a facility should be provided as a language extension or in the form of libraries. If augmented with SIMD data types and operations on them, a MIMD programming language such as Occam can become a general purpose SIMD-MIMD parallel programming language.

We hope that in the future we shall see standardised parallel architectures and standardised parallel programming languages for them. Parallel software should then be as portable as sequential software is at present.

7.3. Further Work

There is ample scope for further research along the lines presented here. The efficient implementation of graphics techniques on parallel processors always lags behind the discovery of new techniques and this holds true for general purpose parallel processors in particular.

There is a wide variety of useful rendering techniques awaiting efficient implementations on general purpose parallel processors; general anti-aliasing by pre-filtering (perhaps a parallel implementation of the A-buffer [Carp84]) and 3D texture mapping are some examples. Furthermore there are alternative (non-polygonal) models and their associated rendering techniques that have to be considered for implementation on general purpose parallel processors; several researchers are already working on the implementation of such techniques as solid modelling and ray tracing. Once general purpose parallel processor algorithms for an adequate set of graphics techniques have been devised and compared, graphics libraries that encompass these techniques should be constructed in order to facilitate the rapid development of graphics applications on general purpose parallel processors.

Efficient rendering algorithms are usually designed to handle a restricted class of convex polygons; the parallel algorithms of Chapters 3, 4 and 5 can only render trapezia and convex polygons for example. The decomposition of polygons into convex parts is therefore an important operation if our model is composed of non-convex polygons; it is necessary to support this operation efficiently so that the rate at which polygons can be decomposed into convex parts is greater than or equal to the rate at which their convex parts can be rendered. We have not investigated whether sequential polygon decomposition techniques can provide adequate performance and this would be an interesting piece of further work. If necessary, parallel polygon decomposition algorithms should be developed.

In Chapter 3 we saw several rendering applications of the evaluation of linear and non-linear polynomial functions. Constructive Solid Geometry objects are usually defined by polynomials of degree 2. The evaluation of 2nd degree polynomial functions would therefore be useful in rendering such objects. Polynomial function evaluation certainly has a wide range of applications (both in graphics and in other fields) and an investigation into techniques for the efficient evaluation of polynomial functions on general purpose parallel processors would be both interesting and of general utility.

Appendix 1. Implementation of Planar Operations

The following procedures are the implementations of some planar
operations on DisArray. DisArray cycles are enclosed in program
folds. Fold names explain the function of the DisArray cycles.

```
PROC broadcast (VAL INT planar, scalar, pd)
  --"planar" is the address of the Least Significant
  --BitPlane (LSBP) of the planar object being created,
  --"scalar" is the scalar being broadcast (integer
  --assumed here) and "pd" is the number of LSB's of
  --"scalar" that will be broadcast in order to create
  --an equal number of bitplanes.

  INT temp:
  SEQ
    temp := scalar
    SEQ i = 0 FOR pd
      SEQ
        IF
          (temp /\ #1) = 0
            ...bitplane (planar + i) := [0]
          TRUE
            ...bitplane (planar + i) := [1]
        temp := temp >> 1
:
```

```
PROC planar.assignment (VAL INT src, dst, pd)
  --"src" and "dst" are the addresses of the LSBP's
  --of the source and destination planar objects respectively.
  --"pd" is the number of bitplanes of the objects. Notice
  --that Q is one of the planar registers.

  SEQ i = 0 FOR pd
    SEQ
      ...Q := bitplane (src + i)
      ...bitplane (dst + i) := Q
:
```

```
PROC planar.conditional.assignment (VAL INT src, dst, mask, pd)
  --"src", "dst" and "pd" are explained in the comment for
  --planar assignment. "mask" is the address of a planar Boolean
  --which indicates which scalar elements of the destination are
  --to be affected. Q and X are the planar registers.

  SEQ
    ...X := bitplane (mask)
    SEQ i = 0 for pd
      SEQ
        ...bitplane (dst + i) := bitplane (dst + i) /\ (~X)
        ...Q := bitplane (src + i) /\ X
        ...bitplane (dst + i) := bitplane (dst + i) \/ Q
:
```

```
PROC planar.addition (VAL INT src1, src2, dst, pd)
  --"src1", "src2" and "dst" are the addresses of the LSBP's of the two
  --source and the destination planar objects (planar integers
  --assumed here). "pd" is the planar arithmetic precision.
  --bitplane (carry) is used as the planar carry.
  --There is no overflow check.

  SEQ
    ...bitplane (carry) := [0]
    SEQ i = 0 FOR pd
      SEQ
        ...Q,X := bitplane (src1 + i)
        ...Q := Q >< bitplane (src2 + i)     -->< means exclusive OR
        ...Q := Q >< bitplane (carry)
        ...bitplane (carry) := (~Q) /\ bitplane (carry)
        ...X := X /\ bitplane (src2 + i)
        ...bitplane (carry) := X \/ bitplane (carry)
        ...bitplane (dst + i) := Q
:


PROC planar.negation (VAL INT src, dst, pd)
  --2's complement of pd-bitplane planar integer whose LSBP
  --address is "src" is computed and stored in planar integer
  --whose LSBP address is "dst". No overflow check.

  SEQ
    ...X := [0]
    SEQ i = 0 FOR pd
      SEQ
        ...Q := X >< bitplane (src + i)
        ...bitplane (dst + i) := Q
        ...X := X \/ bitplane (src + i)
:


PROC planar.subtraction (VAL INT src1, src2, dst, pd)
  --"src1", "src2" and "dst" are the addresses of the LSBP's of the two
  --source and the destination planar objects (planar integers assumed).
  --"pd" is the planar arithmetic precision. The semantics are:
  --dst (x,y) = src1 (x,y) - src2 (x,y)          | x,y: 0..N-1
  --A pd-bitplane workspace whose LSBP address is "work" is used.
  --No overflow check. There is scope for optimisation by combining
  --the planar negation with the planar addition.

  SEQ
    planar.negation (src2, work, pd)
    planar.addition (src1, work, dst, pd)
:
```

```
PROC planar.multiplication (VAL INT src1, src2, dst, pd)
   --"src1", "src2", "dst" and "pd" have the same meanings as for
   --planar addition. Multiplication is implemented by shift-and-add.
   --"work0", "work1" and "work2" are the addresses of the LSBP's of
   --three planar objects which are used as workspaces: "work0" has
   --2*pd bitplanes while "work1" and "work2" have pd bitplanes.
   --There is scope for optimisation (e.g. by combining the planar
   --addition with the conditional planar assignment).
   --There is no overflow check.

   SEQ
     broadcast (work0, 0, (pd + pd))
     broadcast (work1, 0, pd)
     planar.assignment (src1, (work0 + pd), pd)
     SEQ i = 0 FOR pd
       SEQ
         planar.addition (((work0 + pd) - i), work1, work2, pd)
         planar.conditional.assignment (work2, work1, (src2 + i), pd)
     planar.assignment (work1, dst, pd)
 :


PROC planar.comparison (VAL INT src1, src2, mask, pd)
   --"src1" and "src2" are the addresses of the LSBP's of the
   --planar objects to be compared (planar integers assumed here).
   --"mask" is the address of the planar Boolean result. The semantics:
   --mask (x,y) = 1, src1 (x,y) < src2 (x,y)        | x,y: 0..N-1
   --            = 0, otherwise
   --"work" is the address of the LSBP of a pd-bitplane planar object
   --which is used as workspace. There is no overflow check.

   SEQ
     planar.subtraction (src1, src2, work, pd)     --work := src1 - src2
     ...Q := bitplane ((work + pd) - 1)  --sign plane
     ...bitplane (mask) := Q
 :
```

Appendix 2. Implementation of Control Parallel Clipper

```
PROC clip.top (CHAN in, out)
  --Occam implementation of 1 (of the 6) stages of a clipping
  --pipeline. This stage clips against the TOP clipping plane.


  PROC buffer(CHAN in, out)
    [25]REAL32 x:
    WHILE TRUE
      SEQ
        in ? x
        out ! x
  :


  PROC clip1 (CHAN in, out)

    -- declarations
    VAL max.buff      IS 25:
    VAL sd            IS 0.5 (REAL32):    --sd is S/D

    [max.buff] REAL32 in.buff, out.buff:


    PROC clip.from.buff()
      --clips polygon in in.buff against TOP clipping plane
      --and places result in out.buff
      -- declarations
      INT n, t, i1, i2:
      REAL32 x1, y1, z1, w1, x2, y2, z2, w2, alpha:
      BOOL insidev1, insidev2:

      SEQ
        n := INT ROUND(in.buff[0])            --n is #sides of polygon
        t := n * 4
        SEQ i = 1 FOR 4                        --repeat first vertex as last
          in.buff[t + i] := in.buff[i]
        x2 := in.buff[1]
        y2 := in.buff[2]
        z2 := in.buff[3]
        w2 := in.buff[4]
        i1 := 5           --index to input buffer
        i2 := 1           --index to output buffer
        t := 0            --output polygon vertex counter

        SEQ i = 0 FOR n
          SEQ
            -- clip side i
            x1 := x2
            y1 := y2
            z1 := z2
            w1 := w2

            x2 := in.buff[i1]
            y2 := in.buff[i1+1]
            z2 := in.buff[i1+2]
```

```
    w2 := in.buff[i1+3]
    i1 := i1 + 4

    insidev1 := (y1 <= w1)
    insidev2 := (y2 <= w2)

    IF
      (insidev1 AND insidev2)
        -- both vertices inside
        SEQ
          out.buff[i2] := x2
          out.buff[i2+1] := y2
          out.buff[i2+2] := z2
          out.buff[i2+3] := w2
          i2 := i2 + 4
          t := t + 1

      (insidev1 AND (NOT insidev2))
        -- only v1 inside
        SEQ
          --calculate intersection
          alpha := (y1 - w1) / ((y1 - w1) - (y2 - w2))
          out.buff[i2] := x1 + (alpha * (x2 - x1))  --intersect. x
          out.buff[i2+1] := y1 + (alpha * (y2 - y1))  --inters. y
          out.buff[i2+2] := z1 + (alpha * (z2 - z1))  --inters. z
          out.buff[i2+3] := out.buff[i2+2] * sd        --inters. w
          i2 := i2 + 4
          t := t + 1

      ((NOT insidev1) AND insidev2)
        -- only v2 inside
        SEQ
          --calculate intersection
          alpha := (y1 - w1) / ((y1 - w1) - (y2 - w2))
          out.buff[i2] := x1 + (alpha * (x2 - x1))   --inters. x
          out.buff[i2+1] := y1 + (alpha * (y2 - y1))  --inters. y
          out.buff[i2+2] := z1 + (alpha * (z2 - z1))  --inters. z
          out.buff[i2+3] := out.buff[i2+2] * sd        --inters. w
          i2 := i2 + 4

          --place v2 in output buffer
          out.buff[i2] := x2
          out.buff[i2+1] := y2
          out.buff[i2+2] := z2
          out.buff[i2+3] := w2
          i2 := i2 + 4
          t := t + 2

      TRUE
        SKIP



out.buff[0] := REAL32 ROUND (t)
```

```
    WHILE TRUE
      SEQ
        in ? in.buff
        clip.from.buff()
        out ! out.buff
  :


  CHAN  c1, c2:

  PRI PAR
    buffer(in, c1)
    buffer(c2, out)
    clip1 (c1, c2)
  :
```

Appendix 3. Implementation of Data Parallel Clipper

```
C SIMD IMPLEMENTATION OF THE SUTHERLAND-HODGMAN CLIPPER. USES REALS
C CLIPS AGAINST TOP CLIPPING PLANE ONLY
      ENTRY SUBROUTINE DAPCLIP
      REAL *4 VERTEXX(,,10), VERTEXY(,,10)
      REAL *4 VERTEXZ(,,10), VERTEXW(,,10)
      REAL *4 FIRSTVERTEXX(,), FIRSTVERTEXY(,)
      REAL *4 FIRSTVERTEXZ(,), FIRSTVERTEXW(,)
      REAL *4 INTERSECTIONX(,,10), INTERSECTIONY(,,10)
      REAL *4 INTERSECTIONZ(,,10), INTERSECTIONW(,,10)
      REAL *4 ALPHA(,), SD(,)

      INTEGER *4 N(,), V, I, MAXVERT, MAXVERT2

      LOGICAL INSIDEV1(,), INSIDEV2(,)
      LOGICAL LAST(,), M(,), EXTRAVERTEX(,,10)

C INITIALISATIONS
C ASSUME VERTEX ARRAYS AND N (NUMBER OF VERTICES IN EACH POLYGON)
C HAVE BEEN INITIALISED


C SD is S/D
      SD = MAT(0.5)

      MAXVERT = MAXV(N)

      FIRSTVERTEXX = VERTEXX(,,1)
      FIRSTVERTEXY = VERTEXY(,,1)
      FIRSTVERTEXZ = VERTEXZ(,,1)
      FIRSTVERTEXW = VERTEXW(,,1)

      DO 60 V = 1,MAXVERT
      EXTRAVERTEX(,,V) = MAT(.FALSE.)
   60 CONTINUE

C    MAIN BODY
      DO 10 I = 1,MAXVERT

C   REPEAT FIRST VERTEX AS LAST WHERE NECESSARY
      LAST = MAT(I) .EQ. N
      VERTEXX(LAST,I+1) = FIRSTVERTEXX
      VERTEXY(LAST,I+1) = FIRSTVERTEXY'
      VERTEXZ(LAST,I+1) = FIRSTVERTEXZ
      VERTEXW(LAST,I+1) = FIRSTVERTEXW

C   CHECK WHETHER Vi AND Vi+1 ARE INSIDE THE TOP CLIPPING BOUNDARY
      INSIDEV1 = VERTEXY(,,I) .LE. VERTEXW(,,I)
      INSIDEV2 = VERTEXY(,,I+1) .LE. VERTEXW(,,I+1)

C CALCULATE INTERSECTION
      ALPHA = ((VERTEXY(,,I) - VERTEXW(,,I)) -
     *(VERTEXY(,,I+1) - VERTEXW(,,I+1)))
      ALPHA(ALPHA .EQ. 0.0) = MAT(-9999.0)
      ALPHA = (VERTEXY(,,I) - VERTEXW(,,I)) / ALPHA
```

```
      INTERSECTIONX(,,I) = VERTEXX(,,I) +
     *ALPHA * (VERTEXX(,,I+1) - VERTEXX(,,I))
      INTERSECTIONY(,,I) = VERTEXY(,,I) +
     *ALPHA * (VERTEXY(,,I+1) - VERTEXY(,,I))
      INTERSECTIONZ(,,I) = VERTEXZ(,,I) +
     *ALPHA * (VERTEXZ(,,I+1) - VERTEXZ(,,I))
      INTERSECTIONW(,,I) = INTERSECTIONZ(,,I) * SD


      M = (.NOT. INSIDEV1) .AND. INSIDEV2
      VERTEXX(M,I) = INTERSECTIONX(,,I)
      VERTEXY(M,I) = INTERSECTIONY(,,I)
      VERTEXZ(M,I) = INTERSECTIONZ(,,I)
      VERTEXW(M,I) = INTERSECTIONW(,,I)


      EXTRAVERTEX(,,I) = INSIDEV1 .AND. (.NOT. INSIDEV2)

      M = (.NOT. INSIDEV1) .AND. (.NOT. INSIDEV2)
      VERTEXX(M,I) = MAT(-9999.0)
   10 CONTINUE


C  INSERT OVERFLOW (INTERSECTION) VERTICES
C  AT LEAST 2*MAXVERT SPACE MUST BE AVAILABLE IN VERTEX ARRAYS
      MAXVERT2 = 2*MAXVERT
      DO 20 V=1,MAXVERT
      M = EXTRAVERTEX(,,(MAXVERT+1)-V)
      IF (V .EQ. 1) GO TO 25
      DO 30 I=(MAXVERT-V), (MAXVERT+V)-3
      VERTEXX(M,MAXVERT2-I) = VERTEXX(,,(MAXVERT2-1)-I)'
      VERTEXY(M,MAXVERT2-I) = VERTEXY(,,(MAXVERT2-1)-I)
      VERTEXZ(M,MAXVERT2-I) = VERTEXZ(,,(MAXVERT2-1)-I)
      VERTEXW(M,MAXVERT2-I) = VERTEXW(,,(MAXVERT2-1)-I)
   30 CONTINUE

   25 VERTEXX(M,(MAXVERT+2)-V) = INTERSECTIONX(,,(MAXVERT+1)-V)
      VERTEXY(M,(MAXVERT+2)-V) = INTERSECTIONY(,,(MAXVERT+1)-V)
      VERTEXZ(M,(MAXVERT+2)-V) = INTERSECTIONZ(,,(MAXVERT+1)-V)
      VERTEXW(M,(MAXVERT+2)-V) = INTERSECTIONW(,,(MAXVERT+1)-V)
      N(M) = N + MAT(1)
   20 CONTINUE

      MAXVERT = MAXV(N)


C  REMOVE DELETED VERTICES
      DO 40 V = 1,MAXVERT
      M = VERTEXX(,,V) .EQ. MAT(-9999.0)
      IF (V .EQ. MAXVERT) GO TO 45
      DO 50 I=V,MAXVERT-1
      VERTEXX(M,I) = VERTEXX(,,I+1)
      VERTEXY(M,I) = VERTEXY(,,I+1)
      VERTEXZ(M,I) = VERTEXZ(,,I+1)'
      VERTEXW(M,I) = VERTEXW(,,I+1)
   50 CONTINUE
   45 N(M) = N - MAT(1)
   40 CONTINUE

      RETURN
      END
```

References

[Akel88] Akeley K. & T. Jermoluk, "High-Performance Polygon Rendering", Computer Graphics, 22(4), August 1988, pp. 239-246.

[Asan83] Asano T. & T. Asano, "Minimum Partition of Polygonal Regions into Trapezoids", Proceedings 24th Annual Symposium on Foundations of Computer Science, 1983.

[Bres65] Bresenham J.E., "Algorithm for Computer Control of a Digital Plotter", IBM Syst. Journal 4(1), January 1965.

[Carp84] Carpenter L., "The A-buffer, an Antialiased Hidden Surface Method", ACM Computer Graphics, 18(3), July 1984, pp. 103-108.

[Clar80] Clark J.H. & M.R. Hannah, "Distributed Processing in a High-Performance Smart Image Memory", Lambda, 4th quarter 1980, pp. 40-45.

[Clar82] Clark J.H., "The Geometry Engine: A VLSI Geometry System for Graphics", Computer Graphics, 16(3), July 1982, pp. 127-133.

[Cohe81] Cohen D. & Demetrescu S., "A VLSI Approach to Computer Image Generation", Information Sciences Institute, University of Southern California, 1981.

[Crow77] Crow F., "The Aliasing Problem in Computer-Generated Shaded Images", Comm. ACM, 20(11), November 1977, pp. 799-805.

[Crow81] Crow F., "A Comparison of Antialiasing Techniques", IEEE Computer Graphics & Applications, 1(1), January 1981, pp. 40-48.

[Deme85] Demetrescu S., "High Speed Image Rasterization Using Scan Line Access Memories", Proc. 1985 Chapel Hill Conference on VLSI, Computer Science Press.

[Flyn66] Flynn M.J., "Very High-Speed Computing Systems", Proceedings of the IEEE, Vol. 54, 1966, pp. 1901-1909.

[Fole83] Foley J.D. & A. Van Dam, "Fundamentals of Interactive Computer Graphics", Addison-Wesley, 1983.

[Form85] Forman S., "Dynamic Video RAM Snaps the Bond Between Memory and Screen Refresh", Electronic Design, May 30 1985, pp. 117-125.

[Fuch77] Fuchs H., "Distributing a Visible Surface Algorithm over Multiple Processors", Proc. 1977 Annual ACM Conference, October 1977, pp. 449-451.

[Fuch79] Fuchs H. & B. Johnson, "An Expandable Multiprocessor Architecture for Video Graphics", Proc. 6th ACM-IEEE Symposium on Computer Architecture, 1979, pp. 58-67.

[Fuch81] Fuchs H. & J. Poulton, "Pixel-Planes: A VLSI-Oriented Design for a Raster Graphics Engine", VLSI Design, 3rd quarter 1981, pp. 20-28.

[Fuch85] Fuchs H., J. Goldfeather, J.P. Hultquist, S. Spach, J.D. Austin, F.P. Brooks, J.G. Eyles & J. Poulton, "Fast Spheres, Shadows, Textures, Transparencies and Image Enhancements in Pixel-Planes", ACM Computer Graphics, 19(3), July 1985, pp. 111-120.

[Gold86a] Goldfeather J. & H. Fuchs, "Quadratic Surface Rendering on a Logic-Enhanced Frame-Buffer Memory", IEEE Computer Graphics and Applications, 6(1), January 1986, pp. 48-59.

[Gold86b] Goldfeather J., J.P. Hultquist, & H. Fuchs, "Fast Constructive Solid Geometry Display in the Pixel-Powers Graphics System", Computer Graphics, 20(4), August 1986, pp. 107-116.

[Gour71] Gouraud, H., "Continuous Shading of Curved Surfaces", IEEE Transactions on Computers C-20(6), June 1971, pp. 623-628.

[Gree83] Greene D.H., "The Decomposition of Polygons into Convex Parts", Advances in Computing Research, Vol. 1, JAI Press, 1983, pp. 235-259.

[Grim79] Grimsdale R.L., A.A. Hadjiaslanis & P.J. Willis, "Zone Management Processor: A Module for Generating Surfaces in Raster-Scan Colour Displays", Computers and Digital Techniques, 2(1), February 1979, pp. 20-25.

[Gupt81a] Gupta S., "Architectures and Algorithms for Parallel Updates of Raster-Scan Displays", Tech. Rep. CMU-CS-82-111, Computer Science Dept., Carnegie-Mellon University, Pittsburgh, Pa, Dec. 1981.

[Gupt81b] Gupta S., R.F. Sproull & I.E. Sutherland, "A VLSI Architecture for Updating Raster-Scan Displays", Computer Graphics, 15(3), August 1981, pp. 71-78.

[Gutt86] Guttag K., J. Van Aken & M. Asal, "Requirements for a VLSI Graphics Processor", IEEE Computer Graphics & Applications, January 1986, pp. 32-47.

[Hamm77] Hamming R.W., "Digital Filters", Prentice-Hall, Englewood Cliffs, N.J., 1977.

[Hear86] Hearn D. & M.P. Baker, "Computer Graphics", Prentice-Hall International, 1986.

[Hoar85] Hoare C.A.R., "Communicating Sequential Processes", Prentice-Hall, 1985.

[Hock81] Hockney R.W. & C.R. Jesshope, "Parallel Computers", Adam Hilger, 1981.

[Hubb85] Hubbard R.E. & D. Fincham, "Shaded Molecular Surface Graphics on a Highly Parallel Computer", Journal of Molecular Graphics, 3(1), March 1985, pp. 12-14.

[ICL80] "DAP: Introduction to FORTRAN Programming", ICL, 60 Portman Rd, Reading, Berks RG3 1NR, U.K., 1980 Edition.

[ICL81] "DAP: FORTRAN Language", ICL, April 1981.

[INMO84] "OCCAM Programming Manual", INMOS Ltd, 1000 Aztec West, Almondsbury, Bristol BS12 4SQ, U.K., 1984.

[INMO86] "Transputer Reference Manual", INMOS Ltd, October 1986.

[INMO87] "OCCAM 2 Language Definition", INMOS Ltd, February 1987.

[Jess84] Jesshope C.R., "A Reconfigurable Processor Array for VLSI", Supercomputers and Parallel Computation, D.J. Paddon Ed., Oxford University Press, 1984.

[Kauf87] Kaufman A., "An Algorithm for 3D Scan-Conversion of Polygons", Eurographics 1987, published by North-Holland.

[Kilg85] Kilgour A., "Parallel Architectures for High Performance Graphics Systems", NATO ASI Series, Vol. F17, 1985.

[Mand82] Mandelbrot B.B., "The Fractal Geometry of Nature", Freeman, San Francisco, 1982.

[May87] May D. & R. Shepherd, "Communicating Process Computers", Technical Note 22, INMOS Ltd, 1000 Aztec West, Almonsbury, Bristol BS12 4SQ, U.K., February 1987.

[Newe72] Newell M.E., R.G. Newell & T.L. Sancha, "A Solution to the Hidden Surface Problem", Proc. ACM National Conf., 1972, pp. 443-450.

[Newm79] Newman W.M. & R.F. Sproull, "Principles of Interactive Computer Graphics", McGraw Hill, 1979.

[Page83] Page I., "DisArray: A 16×16 RasterOp Processor", Eurographics 1983, pp. 367-381.

[Page88] Page I., "Graphics + Vision = SIMD + MIMD: A Novel Dual Paradigm Approach", Proc. Parallel Processing for Computer Vision and Display, Leeds, U.K., January 1988, to be published by Addison-Wesley.

[Park80] Parke F.I., "Simulation and Expected Performance Analysis of Multiple Processor Z-Buffer Systems", Computer Graphics, 14(3), July 1980, pp. 48-56.

[Park83] Parkinson D., "The Distributed Array Processor (DAP)", Computer Physics Communications, 28, 1983, pp. 325-336.

[Park85] Park C.S., "Interactive Microcomputer Graphics", Addison-Wesley, 1985.

[Phon75] Phong B.T., "Illumination for Computer Generated Pictures", Comm. ACM, 18(6), June 1975, pp. 311-317.

[Redd73] Reddaway S.F., "DAP-A Distributed Array Processor", 1st Annual Symposium on Computer Architecture, Gainesville, Fa, 1973, pp. 61-65.

[Redd88] Reddaway S.F., "Mapping Images onto Processor Array Hardware", in Parallel Architectures and Computer Vision, Edited by I. Page, Oxford University Press, 1988.

[Slot62] Slotnick D.L., W.C. Borck & R.C. McReynolds, "The SOLOMON Computer", AFIPS Conf. Proc. 22, 1962, pp. 97–107.

[Spro82] Sproull R.F., "Using Program Transformations to Derive Line Drawing Algorithms", ACM Trans. on Graphics 1(4), October 1982.

[Spro83] Sproull R.F., I.E. Sutherland, A. Thompson, S. Gupta & C. Minter, "The 8×8 Display", ACM Transactions on Graphics, 2(1), Jan. 1983, pp. 32–56.

[Suth63] Sutherland I.E., "Sketchpad: A Man-Machine Graphical Communication System", Technical Report 296, Lincoln Laboratory, M.I.T., Lexington, Massachussetts, January 1963.

[Suth65] Sutherland I.E., "The Ultimate Display", Proc. IFIP Congress, Vol. 2, 1965.

[Suth74a] Sutherland I.E., R.F. Sproull & R.A. Shumacker, "A Characterisation of Ten Hidden Surface Algorithms", Computing Surveys, 6(1), March 1974, pp. 1–55.

[Suth74b] Sutherland I.E., & G.W. Hodgman, "Reentrant Polygon Clipping", Comm. ACM, 17(1), January 1974, pp. 32–42.

[Theo85] Theoharis T., "Exploiting Parallelism in the Graphics Pipeline", Technical Monograph PRG-54, Oxford University Computing Laboratory, 1985.

[Theo87] Theoharis T. & I. Page, "Parallel Polygon Rendering with Precomputed Surface Patches", Eurographics 1987, published by North-Holland. (This paper is based on the contents of Chapter 4).

[Theo88] Theoharis T. & I. Page, "Incremental Polygon Rendering on a SIMD Processor Array", Computer Graphics Forum, 7(4), 1988, pp. 331–341. (This paper is based on the contents of Chapter 3).

[Theo89a] Theoharis T. & I. Page, "Polygon Rendering on a Dual-Paradigm Parallel Processor", Computers & Graphics, 13(2), 1989, to appear. (This paper is based on the contents of Chapter 5).

[Theo89b] Theoharis T. & I. Page, "Two Parallel Methods for Polygon Clipping", Computer Graphics Forum, 8(2), 1989, to appear. (This paper is based on the contents of Chapter 6).

[Whit80] Whitted T., "An Improved Illumination Model for Shaded Display", Comm. ACM, 23(6), June 1980, pp. 343–349.

[Will77] Willis P.J., "A Real Time Hidden Surface Technique", The Computer Journal, 20(4), 1977, pp. 335–339.

[Will78] Willis P.J., "Proximity Techniques for Hidden-Surface Removal", Computers and Digital Techniques, 1(4), October 1978, pp. 171–178.

[Wind86] Winder C.P., "Transputer Upgrade of the DisArray Graphics Processor", M.Sc. Thesis, Oxford University Computing Laboratory, September 1986.

[Wind87]   Winder C.P., "The Birth of the Disputer", Oxford University Computing
Laboratory, September 1987.

[Wind88]   Winder C.P., "Parallel Processing with the Disputer", Proc. 8th OCCAM User
Group Meeting, Sheffield, U.K., March 1988, published by INMOS.

Vol. 324: M.P. Chytil, L. Janiga, V. Koubek (Eds.), Mathematical Foundations of Computer Science 1988. Proceedings. IX, 562 pages. 1988.

Vol. 325: G. Brassard, Modern Cryptology. VI, 107 pages. 1988.

Vol. 326: M. Gyssens, J. Paredaens, D. Van Gucht (Eds.), ICDT '88. 2nd International Conference on Database Theory. Proceedings, 1988. VI, 409 pages. 1988.

Vol. 327: G.A. Ford (Ed.), Software Engineering Education. Proceedings, 1988. V, 207 pages. 1988.

Vol. 328: R. Bloomfield, L. Marshall, R. Jones (Eds.), VDM '88. VDM – The Way Ahead. Proceedings, 1988. IX, 499 pages. 1988.

Vol. 329: E. Börger, H. Kleine Büning, M.M. Richter (Eds.), CSL '87. 1st Workshop on Computer Science Logic. Proceedings, 1987. VI, 346 pages. 1988.

Vol. 330: C.G. Günther (Ed.), Advances in Cryptology – EURO-CRYPT '88. Proceedings, 1988. XI, 473 pages. 1988.

Vol. 331: M. Joseph (Ed.), Formal Techniques in Real-Time and Fault-Tolerant Systems. Proceedings, 1988. VI, 229 pages. 1988.

Vol. 332: D. Sannella, A. Tarlecki (Eds.), Recent Trends in Data Type Specification. V, 259 pages. 1988.

Vol. 333: H. Noltemeier (Ed.), Computational Geometry and its Applications. Proceedings, 1988. VI, 252 pages. 1988.

Vol. 334: K.R. Dittrich (Ed.), Advances in Object-Oriented Database Systems. Proceedings, 1988. VII, 373 pages. 1988.

Vol. 335: F.A. Vogt (Ed.), CONCURRENCY 88. Proceedings, 1988. VI, 401 pages. 1988.

Vol. 336: B.R. Donald, Error Detection and Recovery in Robotics. XXIV, 314 pages. 1989.

Vol. 337: O. Günther, Efficient Structures for Geometric Data Management. XI, 135 pages. 1988.

Vol. 338: K.V. Nori, S. Kumar (Eds.), Foundations of Software Technology and Theoretical Computer Science. Proceedings, 1988. X, 520 pages. 1988.

Vol. 339: M. Rafanelli, J.C. Klensin, P. Svensson (Eds.), Statistical and Scientific Database Management. Proceedings, 1988. IX, 454 pages. 1989.

Vol. 340: G. Rozenberg (Ed.), Advances in Petri Nets 1988. VI, 439 pages. 1988.

Vol. 341: S. Bittanti (Ed.), Software Reliability Modelling and Identification. VII, 209 pages. 1988.

Vol. 342: G. Wolf, T. Legendi, U. Schendel (Eds.), Parcella '88. Proceedings, 1988. 380 pages. 1989.

Vol. 343: J. Grabowski, P. Lescanne, W. Wechler (Eds.), Algebraic and Logic Programming. Proceedings, 1988. 278 pages. 1988.

Vol. 344: J. van Leeuwen, Graph-Theoretic Concepts in Computer Science. Proceedings, 1988. VII, 459 pages. 1989.

Vol. 345: R.T. Nossum (Ed.), Advanced Topics in Artificial Intelligence. VII, 233 pages. 1988 (Subseries LNAI).

Vol. 346: M. Reinfrank, J. de Kleer, M.L. Ginsberg, E. Sandewall (Eds.), Non-Monotonic Reasoning. Proceedings, 1988. XIV, 237 pages. 1989 (Subseries LNAI).

Vol. 347: K. Morik (Ed.), Knowledge Representation and Organization in Machine Learning. XV, 319 pages. 1989 (Subseries LNAI).

Vol. 348: P. Deransart, B. Lorho, J. Maluszyński (Eds.), Programming Languages Implementation and Logic Programming. Proceedings, 1988. VI, 299 pages. 1989.

Vol. 349: B. Monien, R. Cori (Eds.), STACS 89. Proceedings, 1989. VIII, 544 pages. 1989.

Vol. 350: A. Törn, A. Žilinskas, Global Optimization. X, 255 pages. 1989.

Vol. 351: J. Díaz, F. Orejas (Eds.), TAPSOFT '89. Volume 1. Proceedings, 1989. X, 383 pages. 1989.

Vol. 352: J. Díaz, F. Orejas (Eds.), TAPSOFT '89. Volume 2. Proceedings, 1989. X, 389 pages. 1989.

Vol. 354: J.W. de Bakker, W.-P. de Roever, G. Rozenberg (Eds.), Linear Time, Branching Time and Partial Order in Logics and Models for Concurrency. VIII, 713 pages. 1989.

Vol. 355: N. Dershowitz (Ed.), Rewriting Techniques and Applications. Proceedings, 1989. VII, 579 pages. 1989.

Vol. 356: L. Huguet, A. Poli (Eds.), Applied Algebra, Algebraic Algorithms and Error-Correcting Codes. Proceedings, 1987. VI, 417 pages. 1989.

Vol. 357: T. Mora (Ed.), Applied Algebra, Algebraic Algorithms and Error-Correcting Codes. Proceedings, 1988. IX, 481 pages. 1989.

Vol. 358: P. Gianni (Ed.), Symbolic and Algebraic Computation. Proceedings, 1988. XI, 545 pages. 1989.

Vol. 359: D. Gawlick, M. Haynie, A. Reuter (Eds.), High Performance Transaction Systems. Proceedings, 1987. XII, 329 pages. 1989.

Vol. 360: H. Maurer (Ed.), Computer Assisted Learning – ICCAL '89. Proceedings, 1989. VII, 642 pages. 1989.

Vol. 361: S. Abiteboul, P.C. Fischer, H.-J. Schek (Eds.), Nested Relations and Complex Objects in Databases. VI, 323 pages. 1989.

Vol. 362: B. Lisper, Synthesizing Synchronous Systems by Static Scheduling in Space-Time. VI, 263 pages. 1989.

Vol. 363: A.R. Meyer, M.A. Taitslin (Eds.), Logic at Botik '89. Proceedings, 1989. X, 289 pages. 1989.

Vol. 364: J. Demetrovics, B. Thalheim (Eds.), MFDBS 89. Proceedings, 1989. VI, 428 pages. 1989.

Vol. 365: E. Odijk, M. Rem, J.-C. Syre (Eds.), PARLE '89. Parallel Architectures and Languages Europe. Volume I. Proceedings, 1989. XIII, 478 pages. 1989.

Vol. 366: E. Odijk, M. Rem, J.-C. Syre (Eds.), PARLE '89. Parallel Architectures and Languages Europe. Volume II. Proceedings, 1989. XIII, 442 pages. 1989.

Vol. 367: W. Litwin, H.-J. Schek (Eds.), Foundations of Data Organization and Algorithms. Proceedings, 1989. VIII, 531 pages. 1989.

Vol. 368: H. Boral, P. Faudemay (Eds.), IWDM '89, Database Machines. Proceedings, 1989. VI, 387 pages. 1989.

Vol. 369: D. Taubner, Finite Representations of CCS and TCSP Programs by Automata and Petri Nets. X. 168 pages. 1989.

Vol. 370: Ch. Meinel, Modified Branching Programs and Their Computational Power. VI, 132 pages. 1989.

Vol. 371: D. Hammer (Ed.), Compiler Compilers and High Speed Compilation. Proceedings, 1988. VI, 242 pages. 1989.

Vol. 372: G. Ausiello, M. Dezani-Ciancaglini, S. Ronchi Della Rocha (Eds.), Automata, Languages and Programming. Proceedings, 1989. XI, 788 pages. 1989.

Vol. 373: T. Theoharis, Algorithms for Parallel Polygon Rendering. VIII, 147 pages. 1989.